Perfect
in
Christ

Trading the Burden of Enough
for the Beauty of Sufficient

Perfect
in
Christ

Trading the Burden of Enough
for the Beauty of Sufficient

Michelle Wilson

CFI
An imprint of Cedar Fort, Inc.
Springville, Utah

Paperback ISBN 13: 978-1-4621-4814-1
eBook ISBN 13: 978-1-4621-4815-8

Published by CFI, an imprint of Cedar Fort, Inc.
2373 W. 700 S., Suite 100, Springville, UT 84663
Distributed by Cedar Fort, Inc., www.cedarfort.com

Library of Congress Cataloging Number: 2024936345

Cover design by Shawnda Craig
Cover design © 2024 Cedar Fort, Inc.
Edited by Evelyn Nichols and Kyle Lund
Typeset by Evelyn Nichols

Printed in the United States of America

10 9 8 7 6 5 4 3 2 1

Printed on acid-free paper

For my grandmothers, strong
women who loved God and me.

Jane Shirley Steed
and
Joyce LaVerne Parker

Acknowledgments

Writing a book is never a solo endeavor. I want to thank my advanced readers for their valuable support and feedback on one or more chapters of the book: S. Paul Steed, Alayna Efnor, Emily Flynn, Carol Freebairn, Dennis Gaunt, Donna Hatch, Meghan Hoesch, Amelia Kynaston, Crystal Young, Nancy Mackley, Jenson Parrish, Amryn Scott, Carrie Snider, Holly Steed, and Deanna Young. A special thanks goes to Jenna Livingston, Leann Forsyth, and Miranda Quinton for reading the book in its entirety and offering fantastic support and insight. One more special thank you goes to my big brother, Bob Steed, who helped in a pinch and then said nice things that made me cry.

A huge thank you goes to Lisa Roper and Celia Barnes, who saw beauty in the principle of sufficient and encouraged me to publish the book. A special gratitude belongs to Dru Huffaker and all the good people at Cedar Fort Publishing and Media who opened their arms wide to take me and this book in, edit it, and create a beautiful cover and design. I would especially like to thank Kyle Lund, who went over and above to make this book shine.

I'm also immensely grateful for my husband, Jerey Wilson, for his unfaltering support, to my kids for their grace with me, and to my friends were sounding boards and lunch dates.

As always, the greatest gratitude goes to my Father in Heaven, who planted the seed of sufficient in my heart one April morning because He knew how much I needed it.

Contents

Part One: Our Sufficient

Chapter 1:   The Burden of Enough 1

Chapter 2:   The Beauty of Sufficient 13

Chapter 3:   Sufficient Hope 27

Chapter 4:   Sufficient Faith 41

Chapter 5:   Sufficient Humility 55

Chapter 6:   Sufficient Repentance 69

Part Two: Their Sufficient

Chapter 7:   Sufficient Grace 85

Chapter 8:   Sufficient Strength 107

Chapter 9:   Sufficient Remembrance 127

About the Author 133

PART ONE:
Our Sufficient

CHAPTER 1
The Burden of Enough

TRUTH HAS A WAY OF CHANGING US. ESPECIALLY UNEXPECTED TRUTHS. One of the most powerful stories I've experienced, spoken on, and written about happened one night a few years ago. I don't remember the exact time or date. I don't remember what I was wearing. But, I clearly remember a few things: where I was, who I was with, and the truth God spoke to me that sparked my long-time shift from the burden of enough to the beauty of sufficient.

A few years ago, my young adult daughter and I were discussing her upcoming goals, plans, and expectations. The early twenties can be a challenging time as these new adults try to navigate the transition from teen to adulthood, from dependent to independent. It can be difficult for parents as well. We teeter on a tightrope, balancing between offering advice and giving them space to make their own choices, not to mention practicing the art of accepting and loving your children when they make choices different than you'd have them make. It's a balance I am still trying to master with a lot of prayer and copious amounts of chocolate.

During our conversation, I was doing all I could to keep that balance, to gauge what she needed from me and how I could help. It was difficult because sometimes she didn't want answers, and other times she wanted me to tell her exactly what to do. This time, she'd come to me for guidance, and I wanted to give her what she needed. So, I prayed silently as I listened to her. I knew that with God's help, I could be enough for her. I gave it my best effort. I said so many wonderfully helpful and encouraging things. Still, she walked out of the room crying, and I sat alone with the reality that, once again, I had failed. I wasn't enough.

I laid my head on my desk and I prayed again, apologizing for my weakness and lamenting my not-enoughness. Finally, as the tears fell, I whispered, "Heavenly Father, I am simply not enough for my daughter."

I was hoping, pleading for Him to make me feel better. I wanted Him to reassure me I was enough for her, that I wasn't a failure, that I was enough for her and everyone else in my life because that's what I was supposed to be, right? But my daughter's tears were proof I wasn't. It was a burden that pressed forcefully on my soul.

I wonder if you've felt that burden of enough as well. We women have a lot in common: sisterhood, our testimony of Jesus Christ, and our fierce dedication to the ones we love. We easily sacrifice and strive to be all we can and should be for them. But, unfortunately, most of us, if not all of us, have whispered, "*I'm not enough.*"

This whisper can be loud and occasional or quiet and constant. It can sound different to each person—*I'm not as good as her; I'm not the person I should be; I'm not the mom they need,* or the plain old, *I am not enough.* I, myself, have spent many dark nights in prayer struggling with not being enough. It was a desperate plea and a heavy prison that had often led to the demanding yet fruitless pressure and pursuit of perfection. I found the seemingly obligatory quest for *enough* to be soul-crushing.

The burden of this whisper of not being enough is one that I hope I and many others can be rescued from. I'd like to offer an option to consider, but probably not one you might expect.

I propose an escape from the burden of *enough* can be found in setting *enough* aside.

I propose we trade our focus and effort of *doing* or *being* enough for the desire and effort to *have* sufficient—sufficient hope, faith, humility, and repentance.

I think the solution that will bring us relief from the burden we've placed ourselves under is a focus on what we obtain rather than who we are or are not. This is how we will find the peace we so desperately want and need, the peace that our pursuit of *enough* won't give us. The peace that evades so many like me and maybe you.

A few years ago, I created a Facebook group for a project about the lies women believe. Nearly 200 women joined. One day I asked them to share with me the most challenging lies they had struggled with. The top lie, by far was: *I am not enough.*

The women in the group mentioned a lot of other things as well, like, how they feel they've failed God and their families, that they should be further along the path, that they should be able to love more and forgive easier, that they should be more. They berate themselves because they're not better mothers, sisters, wives, friends, co-workers, children, or disciples. Then they're left feeling sad, depressed, and sometimes even ashamed that they aren't better. That they aren't perfect. That they aren't enough.

The study in the Facebook group provided enough material for a complete book, but for this book, I wanted to share one of the major takeaways. Every woman in that group, at one time or another, felt her weaknesses, flaws, mistakes, or her unique personality were proof that they simply weren't enough. They weren't enough for their families, friends, or even God.

It's a struggle shared by millions and a burden that has not gone unnoticed. Thousands of books, articles, TED talks, and social media posts written in a solid effort to ease the burden of *enough* can be found assuring us we truly are enough. Some of the messages are that we don't have to prove ourselves, we don't have to do or be anything different than we are because we *are* enough. It's a warm message, one that I've needed to hear at times in my life. And, in one very important sense, it is true. In one sense, we *are* enough. Being daughters of heavenly parents means we have innate divinity. Just as a tiny acorn already has potential inside it to become a giant oak tree, we have the spiritual DNA inside us right now to become like Heavenly Father and Mother. We are Their children. There is nothing we can do, say, or choose that will change Their love for us. Simply because of who we are—right now—we all have the same opportunity and privilege to become like

Them. We are enough for Them, Their help, Their effort, and Their love. To Them, we are enough.

But, even with this understanding, we can still be haunted by *enough*. With good intentions, we take the understanding of *enough* beyond our divine nature, adding to it our own descriptors: pretty enough, rich enough, patient enough, funny enough, strong enough, skinny enough, worth enough. And when we fall short in any of the self-prescribed areas, it serves as proof, once again, that truly we are not enough.

Then come the self-chastisement, the guilt, and shame, as thieves of light. And oh, how we want the light of being enough. And so, we follow this by repenting for our weakness, for who we are, and we recommit to *do* better, to *be* better.

It is hard work. Worthy work, we feel. But, like crawling up a down-ward-moving escalator, it demands effort while never letting us arrive.

I've had my share of rides on this escalator of *enough*. There have been times I've fallen short of who I could be, who I should be, times when I failed myself, my family, others, and even God and my Savior. The guilt, the shame, and the self-chastisement inevitably press down. Then, in my effort to be enough, I would repent not just for what I lacked, but for *who* I was, and I committed to do better, to be better, to be enough. And then I would try again. It is an exhausting cycle that I and millions of women and men go through over and over and over.

However, my relationship with *enough* has evolved in recent years. Jesus taught us that with God all things are possible,[01] so I thought it was possible for me to be enough, right? And when I realized I couldn't, then I assumed with God's help I could. He could take my weaknesses and turn them into strengths right now. He could change me into who He and others needed me to be.

This was a comforting thought for me—that with God I could be enough for everything and everyone in my life. I knew I'd fall short and not be enough on my own, but I accepted it because I knew that with Him, I *could* be enough. I could be the mother my kids need me to be. I could be the wife I need to be. I could be the speaker and writer publishers and readers need me to be. I could be whatever calling

01   see Mark 10:27.

or assignment leader members need me to be. I could be the friend, mentor, helper, and everything else everyone else needed me to be. I could be enough.

But that night after my daughter left in tears and I confessed to Heavenly Father once again I wasn't enough, the answer He gave me initiated one of the most pivotal moments in my life—the moment I began to truly reconsider *enough*.

Reconsidering Enough

With my daughter in her room crying and me in mine, I prayed and told Him I wasn't enough. I was ready for Heavenly Father to tell me she would be okay, that I was okay. That I was enough.

But He didn't.

Instead, He said, "Yes, Michelle. You are not enough."

I'll admit, my knee-jerk response was, "Wait, what? I'm not enough? Well, that's insensitive."

I mean, He's my heavenly dad. He's *supposed* to make me feel better, right? Like a best friend you call after you've eaten an entire tube of cookie dough who comes up with some magical logic about how it was actually the responsible thing to do. It's completely untrue, but sometimes you just need to hear it is true.

I knew I wasn't enough, but I needed to hear God tell me I was, for my daughter's sake and for mine. So, His answer that I wasn't enough was a surprise. No, it was a shock.

And then, the rest of His answer came: "Dear Daughter, I never intended you to be enough for her. And I won't make you enough for her because your daughter needs more than just you."

A new peace stilled my tears as I pondered His answer. Thoughts began to flow in a direction I'd never expected: *God can give me inspiration regarding my daughter, but He won't give me all the answers because I am not the only source He wants her to turn to. He wants her to turn to her dad, siblings, trusted leaders, friends, and to God Himself. He has prepared and will assist others in providing for my daughter's needs and wants, along with my efforts.*

I wouldn't be enough for my daughter because I was meant to be just part of her enough.

The idea that I wasn't supposed to be enough for her, or anyone else for that matter, had never occurred to me before. I'll admit; it was scary, the thought of turning some of my daughter's needs over to others. But it was also liberating to know that I didn't have to have *all* the answers or say *all* the right things. And it was comforting as I was assured that God truly had it handled, that He had been and would continue to work through me and many others to offer my daughter all that she needs. And how wonderful that is! My daughter needs her dad, she needs others, she needs God, and she needs her Savior—all beautiful parts of her enough.

As I tried to embrace this innovative notion of enough, a new question arose: How do I make sure I am being my "part" of her enough?

The answer came quickly. My part is to love, serve, and teach the best I can. To be a prayerful, good, and kind person who strives for hope, faith, empathy, and charity.

What I love about this shift in the way I defined *enough* is that it extends beyond my relationship with my daughter to my relationship with my husband, friends, callings, co-workers, etc. I am not supposed to be enough for anyone, only be my best part of their enough. I don't have to meet all of everyone's needs. I don't have to do it all. I am not enough, exactly the way I should be.

Breaking Free from Enough

This revelation was powerful. Truth bombs usually are. And it has saved me from many a meltdown. But alone, it hasn't been enough (pun intended) to protect me completely from the *enough* cycle. There have been times since then that the draw to do and be enough have pulled me back in with the force of a tractor beam, dragging me from a healthy place back to the space station of false expectations and tears. Thankfully, Heavenly Father has helped me be more aware of this pull and has even helped me avoid it . . . mostly.

In the summer of 2021, God told me I needed to go back to school and finish my education. It wasn't my favorite idea, but since He has a track record of never being wrong, I applied and registered for a full load of classes for the fall semester. If there is anything that makes you feel not enough it's sitting in a zoom with kids younger than your own as they explain mathematical concepts no one in real life uses.

The following summer, I was in my bishop's office for my ecclesiastical interview—one of the requirements for registration. The interview became a spontaneous therapy session in which I spewed out all things I was expected to do by God, others, and myself, and how overwhelmed I was feeling. My heart felt so low.

He sat quietly and listened and then, with love in his eyes, he said, "That sounds really difficult."

I nodded, because if I were to reply, tears would have come with the words.

He leaned his elbows on the desk and said, "I'm going to do something I haven't done before." He proceeded to tell me he'd been feeling it was time to call a new Relief Society president. "I've prayed about it a number of times," he said, "and your name is the only one that keeps coming to my mind."

My heart dropped even further. I'd served as Relief Society president before. I loved the calling. It was a privilege to serve with God in that way. But it was hard—the most challenging calling I'd had. There was no way God would ask me to this again. Not now.

Before I could spin into panic, my good bishop held his hands up. "I'm not extending a call to you today," he said softly with an almost apologetic laugh. "But, considering everything you're sharing with me, I am veering from the norm and telling you I believe I will be extending the call in September."

I blinked.

He smiled again gently, then told me he wanted me to have time to think about it and counsel with my husband, Jerey, and consider how the calling might fit into my life and if it was something I felt I could do and wanted to do.

I will love this bishop forever for giving me this unorthodox amount of time. I had five weeks to pray and ponder. Five weeks to counsel with my husband. Five weeks to think about what I could and should do. It only took me a few hours to talk and pray about it before

I knew God wanted me to serve this way, and *I* wanted to as well. I felt good about it. Really good.

During this time before the call would be officially extended, I went through all the mental gyrations. I could totally do this! Oh wait, I can't even keep my own head above water, how could I help anyone else not drown? At one point, I began to question my ability, which led to questioning my worth. Could I do enough? Could I *be* enough for this calling? The dreaded burden of *enough* began to pull me into the dark.

This time, however, I decided not to go gently into that bad night. I resisted the pull towards high expectations and low self-esteem. I told myself I wouldn't think or joke about being called a second time so "I'd have a chance to do it right this time." I told myself I wasn't going to invite the adversary or give him an opportunity to pull me back into the "enough" cycle. I was going to have joy in my calling. I committed to give my heart to God and the sisters, not to the quest of being and doing enough.

Breaking free from the pull of enough was not easy. Sometimes I can still feel its power, especially when my plate overflows with school, family, writing, work, calling, and other responsibilities. It can be hard when I *feel* there is more, that I should be more.

This begs a question: If God didn't intend for us to be enough for Him or anyone else, why then do we often have this feeling of "more"? Why do we so often and so deeply feel that we should do or be more? If not to reach *enough*, then to what end?

The Wonderful News

We find the answer in a term coined by Elder Neil A. Maxwell called "divine discontent."[02] It's the innate feeling we have in our souls that there is more to this world than we can see. We are taught we came from the presence of light and God and now we are in a fallen state, only able to feel Him through the Holy Ghost.

Our spirits must be homesick for the feeling of Heaven. This is what they long for, what they understand, that there is more to our

02 Neal A. Maxwell, "Becoming a Disciple," *Ensign,* June 1996.

eternal existence than this mortal world. This is what the gospel is all about—giving us a way to return home in a position to progress even further in light.

I wonder if divine discontent is something we sometimes misinterpret. Our spirits long for the heaven we can't remember, for the heavenly parents and home we can't recall. Our souls instinctively reach for light, for our sacred inheritance. Anything less isn't good enough. Our souls don't want to settle.

Our minds, however, don't know what our souls know. I wonder if we interpret this feeling of wanting more as needing to be more here and now, as if we are lacking somehow—as if we are not enough. The deficiency lies within us, we think. And so, we try to do more, to be more, so we can somehow find what we feel is missing.

Sister Michelle D. Craig spoke eloquently of the power of this instinctive emotion, this divine discontent. She said,

> Each of us, if we are honest, feels a gap between where and who we are, and where and who we want to become. We yearn for greater personal capacity. We have these feelings because we are daughters and sons of God, born with the Light of Christ yet living in a fallen world. These feelings are God given and create an urgency to act.[03]

Sometimes this urgency to act can be hyperextended into the unhealthy effort of *enough*. Sister Craig warned,

> We should welcome feelings of divine discontent that call us a higher way, while recognizing and avoiding Satan's counterfeit—paralyzing discouragement. This is a precious space into which Satan is all too eager to jump. We can choose to walk the higher path that leads us to seek for God and His peace and grace, or we can listen to Satan who bombards us with messages that we will never be enough: rich enough, smart enough, beautiful enough, anything enough. Our discontent can become divine—or destructive.[04]

So, how do we make our discontent divine?
We look to Jesus Christ.

---

03   Michelle D. Craig, *Divine Discontent*, General Conference (Salt Lake City: The Church of Jesus Christ of Latter-day Saints), October 2018, Gospel Library App.
04   Ibid.

Our Savior wants us near Him because He is where we will have peace and growth and joy. He has the power to help us bridge the gap between who we are now and who we can become.

This is why, time and time again, the Savior invites us to follow Him. When He meets a certain ruler who wants eternal life, Jesus says, "follow me."[05] When He sees Simon and Andrew on the water, He calls for them to "follow me."[06] What do we do when we feel don't feel we are enough? How do we make our discontent divine? He gives us the answer: "Come to me."[07]

He invites us to partake of His power, grace, and strength. A way to crawl out from the beneath the burden of *doing* and *being* enough is to direct our hearts to *having* sufficient things that bring us to Him.

This is what our souls want—light, truth, progress, Jesus.

This new way of looking at *enough* started during a session of general conference. The speaker used a word I'd heard a thousand times before, but that day, in that moment, it sounded different. Important.

The word was *sufficient.*

Throughout that weekend, the word didn't leave me. As I pondered what it meant and its relationship to *enough*, I turned to the scriptures.

First, I looked for the times the Lord or his prophets use the word "enough" in relation to who we are or how we should be. I found only one that seemed close. In Matthew chapter ten, Jesus sets the Twelve apart to do as He did. After He gives them direction to travel, teach, and heal, He tells them of the challenges that lie ahead. Then He says, "The disciple is not above his master, nor the servant above his Lord. It is enough for the disciple, that he be as his master, and the servant as his lord."[08]

Here, He is not telling them to be like Him. He is telling them they will be treated as He was—they will be persecuted as He was. (As a side note, I love the six verses that follow where Jesus comforts His apostles, tells them not to be afraid and that they are known and valued. Oh, the love Jesus has for us!)

---

05   Luke 18:22.
06   Matthew 4:19.
07   Matthew 11:28.
08   Mathew 10:24-25.

Nowhere in the scriptures are we told we should *do* or *be* enough for God or anyone else.

A cursory search of the counsel of modern-day prophets found a lack of the same. It seems the burden of *enough* was never ours to carry.

This came as a tremendous relief to me. I had felt the burden of *enough* when I couldn't help my daughter. I felt the press of it when I missed scripture study. I buckled under its weight when my mom died and I couldn't balance my responsibilities in my grief. I wasn't doing or being enough. Maybe you've felt this way too in your calling, your family, or your own mind. I discovered through study and prayer the wonderful understanding that we don't have to do or be enough. That isn't our burden to carry.

I then searched the scriptures for *sufficient.* There I found references about *having* a sufficient amount of the things that bring us to and keep us with the Lord. I realized that this really is what the Lord wants from us. He doesn't want us to do and be enough. He doesn't want or expect us to strive for perfection. He wants us to come unto Him and be perfected *in* Him.[09]

I love that last line. The burden of *enough* puts perfection squarely on our shoulders. We have to try hard. We have to do better. We have to be better. And we do all of these things better and better until we become perfect.

The beauty of *sufficient* is that we are relieved of that false, self-imposed responsibility. Through *sufficient* we come to understand who can perfect us (Jesus Christ) and what being perfect in Him really means.

Over the following weeks of prayer and study, I began to experience peace and relief as I started my own paradigm shift. It wasn't easy. It took work to detach myself from old patterns of thinking and behavior. I'm still working at it. I hope as you read this book, you find relief in the shift as well. I hope you reach for the more our spirits know there is. I hope you can put down the unnecessary burden of *enough*, one thought at a time, expectation at a time, and free your hands to reach for the beauty of sufficient.

---

09   see Moroni 10:32-33.

CHAPTER 2

The Beauty of Sufficient

I KNOW. SUFFICIENT. IT'S NOT A BEAUTIFUL WORD, LIKE "ELOQUENCE" or "serendipity." It doesn't sound like a ground-breaking, earth-shattering answer. But, in the spirit of the gospel, "sufficient" is not only different than enough, it's what is needed. Literally.

We don't read about being enough in the scriptures. However, we *do* read about sufficient, specifically sufficient hope,[10] sufficient faith,[11] sufficient humility,[12] sufficient repentance,[13] sufficient grace,[14] sufficient strength,[15] and sufficient remembrance.[16]

Each of these references speak of a principle or gift that we need for us to come closer to and stay by Heavenly Father and the Savior. This is what They want—not for us to do more or be more, but to *have* what is needed to be by Them so Their grace can work in our lives and in us. That's it.

Let your mind wrap itself around this concept. Let your heart rest in it. You do not have to keep trying to *do* or *be* enough for God, the Savior, yourself, or anyone else around you. You do not have to *be* perfect, or even close to it. This is not about you being like Jesus right now.

---

10   Moroni 7:3.
11   3 Nephi 17:8.
12   Ether 9:35.
13   Alma 24:11.
14   D&C 18:31.
15   Ether 12:27.
16   Alma 5:6.

It's about drawing nearer to Him, putting yourself in the position for His grace to work in and for you.

We do not have to earn our way into His good graces or perform our way into heaven. Our goal is to simply choose the things that keep us by His side—in His presence. He will do the heavy lifting. He already has.

By now I hope I've laid a compelling foundation for why and how we can let go of the burden of enough. But you might be wondering exactly what the difference between enough and sufficient really is. Is it more than just semantics? Yes it is.

Depending on the definitions, *enough* and *sufficient* can be interchangeable in certain situations. For example, "we have enough for our needs" is the same as "we have sufficient for our needs." In fact, in doing a spell check on this book, my software editor kept wanting to change "enough of" to "sufficient."

However, though they can be used interchangeably on occasion, the core of their meanings is different; enough implies that one is meeting a bare minimum. Sufficient, on the other hand, implies fulfilling a need or specific purpose.

God doesn't want us to be enough—the bare minimum. He doesn't even want us to have the bare minimum. God wants us to have everything we need so He can make us everything. This is His purpose, to bring to pass our immortality and eternal life.[17] He isn't in the business of *enough*. He's in the business of perfection, and *sufficient* is how it's done.

Another difference between enough and sufficient is our focus. Even with the best of intentions, a focus on doing or being enough is a *self-centric* pursuit. It's about *us* not failing to be and do what *we* feel *we* should. As we pursue the elusive *enough*, our focus is on our performance and for many of us, our effort to surpass *enough* and arrive at *perfection*.

Sufficient, however, is *Savior-centric*. It's about understanding and obtaining the things that the Savior offers and asks, the things that can bring us closer to Him and allow Him in our lives because *He* is who changes us. Not us. *He* makes us perfect and whole. The pursuit for sufficient is the pursuit to follow Jesus, to invite the power and grace of Jesus Christ through His Atonement to work in our lives. I love how Elder Vern P. Stanfill stated simply that "we are measured by our

---

17   see Moses 1:39.

personal devotion to God that we manifest in our efforts to follow him in faith."[18]

Seeing the difference between a self-centric and Savior-centric view can have a significant impact on our lives. A sweet young adult woman friend of mine named Meghan made the following comment: "The concept of self-centric vs. Savior-centric is unique and beautiful. I like how it makes me think about how I view my needs. When *enough* is my guiding force, I am thinking about how *I* am failing. When *sufficient* is my guide, I am thinking how the Savior is how I am able to accomplish everything. We are bringing the focus back to the Savior, and therefore uniting our thoughts and actions to be more in line with Him."[19]

This is one of the many things I love about the pursuit of sufficient—my attention is on Jesus. My devotion is to God. My prayers are about what I can do to be nearer Them now, not apologize for how I'm failing to be like Them now. My energy is focused on walking, running, and sometimes crawling toward Them. Not walking, running, or crawling towards some expectation I've set for myself.

The Beauty of Sufficient

I recently visited a sweet older Relief Society sister. She was a stalwart ministering sister, primary worker, and temple worker. For the past twenty years, she and her husband had been getting up at 2:30am every Saturday morning, working a full shift at the temple, staying to serve as patrons, then arriving home around 3pm.

I sat at her table eating homemade banana bread and drinking hot chocolate while warmly chatting with her and her ministering sister about life, movies, family, and ministering. After a while, this good sister paused and stroked the table near her cup. She watched her finger rub the plastic tablecloth as she told me that she and her husband had called the temple earlier that day to let them know they were no longer able to be temple workers. Then she looked at me and through a smile, said, "I can use my extra time now to step up my game. I've gotta be

---

18 Stanfill, Vern P., *The Imperfect Harvest*, General Conference (Salt Lake City: The Church of Jesus Christ of Latter-day Saints, April 2023), Gospel Library App.

19 M. Hoesch, personal communication, March 20, 2023.

and do more. I want to make sure I get a good spot in heaven." She laughed softly, but her eyes told me there was a little truth in her jest.

"You don't have to earn your way into heaven," I said.

She shrugged doubtfully.

"Do you have hope in Jesus Christ?" I asked. "Do you have hope that what you've been taught is actually true?"

"Well, yes," she said.

"Do you have some faith?" I asked.

She touched the pendant of her necklace—a mustard seed set beneath a small gold mountain range representing the faith needed to move mountains. "Yes," she answered.

"Are you trying to be humble?"

"Yes. I try."

"Do you repent regularly?"

"Yes, I do."

"Then," I said, "You'll be okay. You do those things now, and God will bless you with the strength and grace you need for a place next to Him now *and* later."

Relief washed over her, and she laughed out loud. "Well, okay then!"

It was a wonderful and revelatory moment for her as she began to realize the simplicity of the gospel and the beauty of *sufficient*. It is simple, achievable, and divine.

When we stop trying to do and be enough and start focusing on having the sufficient things we need in our lives, something wonderful can happen. As we move closer to the Savior, we lose the guilt and shame. Instead, we find opportunities, opportunities to understand, to lay hold of every good thing, to become like Him *through* Him, not through ourselves. We can stop feeling we don't measure up. We can stop apologizing to God for not being perfect and instead repent so we can be nearer to the One who is.

How Much Sufficient Is Sufficient?

I was chatting with someone about the concept of sufficient recently and, more than once, they asked, "How much sufficient is enough?" They wanted a way to measure sufficient so they could tell when they achieved it. I told him, much to his dismay, that it couldn't and shouldn't be measured in the same way we measure the checklist of *enough*. One of the allures of our checklists is the hit of dopamine when we check the box. Read my scriptures, check. Said my prayers, check. Those checks feel good. That's hard to move away from. Even scary. But so are the dangers, two of which are the guilt and shame that come when our boxes remain empty. When we focus on things we can measure, we can invite a sense of self-congratulation or self-flagellation because it is a self-centric pursuit.

Measuring sufficient is different. There are no checkboxes of tasks. No long lists. Just a simple question: in this moment, is my [hope, faith, humility, repentance] moving me toward Jesus Christ? If the answer is yes, then it is sufficient. If the answer is no, then the focus should be on strengthening our [hope, faith, humility, repentance] until it does propel us forward.

What I love about sufficient is that it only takes a part of something to equal the whole because of Jesus. Take tithing as an example. The Lord asks for ten percent of our increase. That's it. Ten percent—only a part of our increase—is sufficient to be a *full* tithe payer. A percentage is sufficient in the Lord's eyes.

The miracle of the loaves and fishes can help us further understand the concept of a part being equal to the full. The Savior, freshly grieving the loss of his cousin, seems to want some time alone. His effort was in vain, for many people—5,000 of them at least—follow Him, hoping for miracles and truth. So, Jesus spends the day with them, teaching profound truths.

After a good amount of time, the people grow hungry. Jesus, in His perfect wisdom, allows His apostles to problem solve with Him. They have money—about six months of wages worth—but that isn't enough to buy bread "sufficient for them, that every one of them may take a little."[20]

Another of Jesus's apostles approaches him with a possible solution. It is far-fetched. In fact, it almost seems useless to suggest. But he does.

---

20   John 6:7.

"There is a lad here," he says, "which hath five barley loaves, and two small fishes: but what are they among so many?"[21]

This is the part I love, the part that I've overlooked for 50 years of my life. It isn't Jesus who provides the loaves and fishes or even His apostles. It is an unnamed young man, a "lad." I wonder if this young man saw a need and offered all he had. Or perhaps the apostles saw this young man's food and requested it. I wonder if he gave up his food thinking he would go hungry himself. We don't know. But, what we do know is that this young man had five loaves of barley bread and two small fishes that he was willing to give to Jesus.

I'm sure he knew it wasn't enough to feed the crowd. Still, he gave what he had to Jesus. His offering was sufficient for Jesus. Then Jesus makes this lad's offering sufficient for all. He and the 5,000 people don't merely get enough to eat; they are "filled,"[22] including, I'm sure, the lad himself.

We can't do it all or be it all. But we *can* have sufficient for *His* purpose, and we can offer our sufficient to Him. Our part can equal the fullness of what He needs—what *we* need—in a given time and place.

We give Him what we have to give and He will do miracles with it, with us.

This is such a relief to me! We don't need to be and do everything ourselves; we just need to have sufficient hope, faith, humility, repentance, and remembrance of the Lord.

Back to my friend's question: how do we know if we have reached a sufficient amount of these things? If your hope, faith, humility, and repentance drive you to make and keep your covenants in that moment in time and come closer to Jesus Christ, they are sufficient.

But, sufficient for what?

Sufficient to be healed, to be strengthened, to be forgiven, to be directed, to be perfected, to be saved. This is the beauty of sufficient. We seek to have a sufficient portion of hope, faith, humility, and repentance, and we can receive the fullness of all He has to offer. It doesn't seem fair, and yet, it's God's plan—His wonderful, merciful plan.

---

21   John 6:9.
22   John 6:12.

Perhaps we could understand and appreciate sufficient if we inched it a little farther away from "enough" and closer to "effective." Our goal is to be closer to the Savior. We seek to have a portion of the things that effectively close the gap between the Savior and ourselves.

Sufficient isn't about an amount; it's about efficacy. Jesus Christ wants us to have hope, faith, humility, and repentance to keep us focused on and moving toward Him.

What does *sufficient* look like? It looks like the woman who touched the hem of Jesus's clothes,[23] the widow's mite,[24] the men who left their nets to follow Him,[25] the young man who searched for ore to build a ship he didn't know how to build,[26] the 2,500 people who waited for their turn to touch the Resurrected Savior.[27] These examples are all different—different circumstances, different sizes, different people. But they are all the same—each one had a sufficient hope, faith, humility, or repentance that drew them nearer to the Lord.

Sufficient isn't a global standard. It is personal, intimate. Powerful.

I've seen the beauty of sufficient all around me. Sufficient looks like my good friend who came to church smelling like cigarettes. It looks like my mother sitting at my bedside when I was hurting. Sufficient looks like my gay friend saying his first prayer in months. It looks like my daughter opening her scriptures to read after a long day of school and work. It looks like my dear friend getting out of bed after she tragically lost her daughter. And it looks like my sweet friend walking into her bishop's office to talk.

Sufficient is effective movement toward God and the Savior. It is beautiful. And it works.

The Symbiotic Relationship of Sufficient

The relationship of sufficient is a symbiotic one. I've mentioned our part—having sufficient hope, faith, humility, and repentance to move us toward God and Jesus Christ. But here is where the miracle comes

23   see Mark 5:24.
24   Mark 24:43-44.
25   Matthew 4:20.
26   1 Nephi 17:9.
27   3 Nephi 3:11.

in. When we move toward Them, we never do it unassisted. We are never alone. The moment we reach for sufficient, we unlock power from heaven.

Amulek taught this powerful truth nearly 2100 years ago.

> Yea, I would that ye would come forth and harden not your hearts any longer; for behold, now is the time and day of your salvation; and therefore, if ye will repent and harden not your hearts, immediately shall the great plan of redemption be brought about unto you.[28]

In sufficient-speak, he said, "Hey, I want you to have sufficient hope and faith to come toward Christ and have sufficient humility, because the time for Him to help you is *now*; and if you repent sufficiently and stay humble, you will *immediately* receive the help you need from God and the Savior through the Atonement to keep moving toward Them."

I love that word, *immediately*.

When our goal is to have sufficient to be near the Savior, we unlock God's opportunity to help us. As we offer our *sufficient* on the table, He meets us with the supernal gifts of grace and strength *now*. Not later when we've proven we've done or become enough. Not later when we've become "worthy" of His love and help. Not later after we've checked all the boxes. But, here, in the moment we choose to feed hope, faith, humility, and repentance—*in that very moment*—He helps us on our path. We make small movements toward Them and They give us monumental help in that effort.

It is the ultimate, divine win/win.

To demonstrate this symbiotic wonder, allow me to share another personal story.

In 2001, after years of suffering from endometriosis, I had a complete hysterectomy. It was a difficult decision. I had always wanted a big family, but we were only able to have two children naturally. It had been four years since my youngest had been born. The pain of the endometriosis (despite having five laparoscopies to clean it out) and side effect of fertility medication made parenting my two little ones difficult. And so, after much prayer, Jerey and I decided to sacrifice having a bigger family later for a better quality of life with the little family we had now.

---

28   Alma 34:31.

A few hours before the surgery, I was in a hospital dressing room changing into my breezy blue gown. Grunting from the dressing room next door told me there was another woman changing as well. After a few more huffs she called out to me, "I'm getting my sinuses cleaned out. What are you in for?"

"A hysterectomy."

"Oh my," said faceless woman, "I had one years ago." Grunt. "Got an infection. Most painful thing I ever felt." Grunt. "Almost died." Huff. Grunt.

I stood there, half dressed in my little room, not sure how to respond. "Um, thank you?" I said. It wasn't the most eloquent response, but how do you answer that?

The surgery went well, and I was home and recovering the next day. I was told I'd start feeling better after the third day. My doctor told me his wife was back to work after a week. So, on the fourth day when I didn't feel better, I began to be annoyed. I'm not a very patient patient. By the tenth day I was getting worse. By the eleventh day, I was pretty bad. I thought I was being weak, a baby. I was tougher than this. So, I pushed myself to do some chores and walk around the house.

On the morning of the twelfth day, Jerey had taken the kids to the park so I could have some quiet time. Pain suddenly tore through my abdomen. I stumbled into the bathroom where I discovered the bleeding. I was hot, clammy. I was exhausted. I cleaned up and somehow got back into my bed. I was sick. Really sick. The woman's words crashed into my mind, and I knew exactly what was wrong.

But here was the problem. I was in so much pain, I was so sick, I was so tired, that I knew there was nothing I could do about it. I did not have it in me to go back to the hospital. I couldn't imagine getting out of bed. I felt my body shutting down.

I began to pray. I talked to God and told Him I was too tired to try. I knew what was coming and I didn't have the energy to fight it. Heavenly Father told me to hang on, that everything would be okay. But I couldn't. I was too tired. There was too much pain. I didn't have it in me. So, I told Him I would be seeing Him again soon, and closed my eyes and gave up.

Just then, Jerey walked into the room. I looked at him and something woke inside me. It was hope. I didn't want to die. I hoped what Heavenly Father had told me was true.

That hope was sufficient to ignite action, which is faith. I reached my hand out toward Jerey and weakly said, "I need a blessing. And then, we have to go to the hospital."

This was all I could offer; all I had in me. But it was sufficient.

He gave me a blessing. My mom stayed with the kids while Jerey took me to the hospital. I barely remember the ride there aside from the pain and vomiting. We got the ER and I was forced to get an ultrasound with a very full bladder. I sobbed. The ultrasound technician gasped.

Ten minutes later Jerey and I were sitting in the doctor's office. Not the white sterile one with the paper-lined table and tools. But the one you see in the movies with the mahogany desk and wooden shelves lined with medical books and family photos. Here the doctor told me I had an infection the size of a dinner plate in my gut. If I had waited just one more hour to come in, I would have died. He needed to operate right now.

Jerey squeezed my hand. I looked at him, prayed, then, through tears, I nodded.

Another sufficient.

I was walked from his fancy office straight into the operating room.

A hand reaching toward my husband, a prayer and a nod, this is what my sufficient looked like, small movements toward God.

At the same time, God gave me the strength to get out of my bed and somehow get to the hospital. Through the gift of grace, I walked into the surgery room a second time. I chose Him and immediately, He helped me. This is the beauty of a symbiotic sufficient relationship.

Three hours later I was in my recovery room. Five days later I was back home. Three weeks later, I was back to normal. Ten years later we adopted our youngest. Twenty-three years later I'm realizing yet another layer of the purpose God can lend to this experience. What I had to offer in that moment wasn't huge or momentous, but it was sufficient to move me toward God's will for me. And He gave me sufficient grace and strength to get there.

Now, not to stray too far from the moving message, but I must share with you another beautiful moment that came from this experience. My husband has always been wonderful. But, when our kids were little, there were parts of my life as a stay-at-home mom he simply didn't understand. On the fourth day of my recovery, Jerey came to visit me in the hospital. My four-year-old son skipped into the room with a smile. My three-year-old daughter sauntered in with a fresh self-made half-mullet. And Jerey straggled in from behind looking as tired as I felt. "I don't get it," he said, shaking his head. "I pick up the floor and go to the next room to quickly grab something. I come back and there is stuff all over the floor. I just cleaned it up. Where does the mess come from? How does this even happen?" My son and half-mullet daughter were grinning. They knew the answer. I knew the answer. And now, because of my infection, my husband was beginning to see the answer. He looked at me and said, "I get it now. What you do is amazing."

I'm pretty sure those magical words played a part in my recovery. Perhaps this was another perk of sufficient? But I digress.

In the last chapter I shared the truth that I wasn't supposed to be enough for my daughter Paige, just part of her enough. Sufficient is similar to that concept. We don't have to have perfect hope, faith, humility, or repentance right now. That isn't possible in our mortal state. What God wants from us is simply a *part* of those things—a sufficient amount that moves us closer to Him. Sufficient is our part of His whole.

It isn't about becoming *like* Them right now, but being *near* Them right now. That is where the magic of change, progression, and conversion happen—in Their presence. We are perfected *in* Them.[29]

A Very Short Note on Perfection

Many of us are painfully aware of Jesus's command to "be ye therefore perfect, even as your Father which is in heaven is perfect."[30] I say painfully, because we often stop at the first mention of *perfect* and attach

---

29   see Moroni 10:32-33.
30   Matthew 5:48.

our current understanding to it. We tell ourselves this must mean Jesus is telling us we need to be flawless like Heavenly Father. Make no mistakes. We need to do and be better, until there is no more room for improvement.

However, the Greek word for perfection used in this verse means something totally different. *Teleios* means complete, completeness, or of full age. Jesus wants us to be whole and fully developed. And the only way to achieve this is to be near Him so His grace can allow that to happen.

Sometimes it's easy to forget or even not realize the end goal. It's not about being perfect, but about becoming a perfect being, our exalted selves. This transformation only happens at the corner of agency and grace—where our sufficient hope, faith, humility, and repentance meet His sufficient strength and grace. This is the place where the magic happens. Though it's not magic at all.

What to Expect

This book is divided into two parts: Our Sufficient and Their Sufficient. In "Part One: Our Sufficient", we're going to explore more deeply the things we are encouraged, even commanded, to have sufficient supply of and effort in—specifically, hope, faith, humility, and repentance. "Part Two: Their Sufficient," will dive deeper into the things They provide for us to be successful in our shared goals—specifically grace and strength. Then, I will end by touching on the importance of sufficient remembrance.

I want to add a caveat here. Having sufficient hope, faith, humility, and repentance does not mean our lives will be free of challenges, trials, and heartache. This mortal life is a full-package deal, and hard and even painful things are included right next to successes, good times, and joy. Woven through all of these is love.

Our search for sufficient doesn't exclude the hard things, but it does allow God to help us through those things. When we have sufficient, we can see purpose in our pain, love in our grief, light in our darkness, softness in our self-analysis, and strength from above. Sufficient doesn't mean a life lived in ease, but a life lived with Jesus Christ.

When I talk with women about toxic perfectionism, I share with them this saying: *Perfection isn't about performance, it's about proximity.* When we focus on the self-centric pursuit of enough, our eyes are drawn to the unreachable goal of perfection in our performance and in ourselves. When we focus on Savior-centric sufficient, our eyes are drawn to the reachable goal of being near the Savior. This is where we will find our peace, our strength, and our perfection.

As I've reconsidered enough and studied sufficient, I have loved the answers I've received and the direction they've sent me in—away from fear, temptations to control, guilt, and shame, and directly toward God and Jesus Christ. I hope your experience with sufficient is similar. I hope as you learn to step away from the self-centric chore of being and doing enough yourself and move toward the Savior-centric pursuit of having sufficient for Him, you will discover a deeper sense of understanding, relief, peace, and joy. I also hope you find a truer sense of purpose and of self.

I hope you begin to see that the "more" you feel you need in your life isn't about you, but about getting more of Him. And the beauty of it all is that He is within our each—a portion of hope, a seed of faith, a desire to be humble, and a habit of repentance are all enough to draw us toward Him.

The fulfillment of our spiritual potential will not happen overnight or even in this mortal lifetime, but we can have moments of progression, effective moments that turn our hearts to Jesus, that bring us closer to Him, and allow us to walk with Him. And when we do, immediately He blesses us with the strength and grace we need to change, to progress, and to become more like Him.

This, my good friends, is God's work and glory. It is the "more" our spirits long for. Our *sufficient* is the key to obtaining His all.

Our sufficient is enough for God. His sufficient is good enough for us.

And that is a beautiful, perfect thing indeed.

CHAPTER 3

Sufficient Hope

I HAVE ALWAYS LOVED HOPE. THE IDEA THAT A SMALL THOUGHT OR desire can give us the courage to walk through fear and fire is powerful. It can lift our eyes and our spirits. It can send us to our knees or down a new path. And, in cases like my old friend Linda,[31] hope can open the door to so much more.

I met Linda in the parking lot of our apartment building when I was a young mother of two. She also had two kids. I felt an instant connection with her. Something just clicked. During our first conversation, we bonded over sleepless nights and crushed Cheerios stuck in our hair. Over the next few weeks, it became apparent our similarities ended there.

Linda was a single mom with two kids by two different men, neither of whom were in the picture now. She'd been raised in an abusive home. As an adult she'd had little contact with her family, and what contact she did have wasn't always good. She worked a waitress job during the day, but it still wasn't enough to make ends meet.

As our friendship grew, she opened up more, and I shared more about the gospel with her. She was interested yet hesitant to believe. Finally, I asked her why. Through tears of shame, she told me that she used to sleep with men for rent money. She hadn't done that for a while. However, her bills were being paid by a man in return for

---

31 Her name has been changed for privacy reasons.

her company. Intimacy, in its full definition, wasn't required, though nearly everything else was. It was demeaning in her eyes.

She wanted a better life for her two girls and was willing to do whatever it took to take care of them. Besides, she felt at this point she didn't deserve anything more. She had no hope for more. Who could love someone who gave herself away for money? Who could love someone even she couldn't love?

In my sheltered life up to that point, I'd never grown close to someone with such a past. I ached for her. I cried with her. At times I had no idea what to say to her. What possibly could I say or do that could help her? All I could do what share with her what had helped me so often in my life.

Hope.

The hope that God was real and that He knew me and loved me. Hope that all I had been taught could be real. Hope that I could love and be loved. Hope that I had an eternal nature and a divine destiny. And hope that I was worth it. This hope pulled me through my doubts and allowed me to choose and exercise faith, to prove that hope wasn't in vain.

I told her there was hope for her, that God loved her, that not only was He her God but her Father in Heaven who loved her unequivocally, deeply, and eternally. I told her I loved her and I respected her. Then we cried together some more.

She'd never fathomed God would love her, let alone love her as His child—especially after what she'd done. But she began to hope—desperately—that it was true. That hope gave her the desire and courage to meet with the missionaries to learn more about her divine nature and heritage.

As we met each week, I was in awe of the change in her. As her hope grew stronger, so did her testimony and her faith. Her smile grew wider and her eyes grew brighter. She learned the principles of the gospel and the Spirit bore witness to her they were true. She marveled that the heavens would open to speak to *her*.

However, what she cherished most of all was her newly found identity as a daughter of God. She was beginning to see who she was, who she really is, and who she could be if she chose to. The understanding growing within her of her purpose—of God's purpose—was powerful and liberating. Self-worth was something she thought she'd never feel again, something she'd lost hope in. And now, for the first time in her adult life, she not only hoped to feel love, but she felt love and felt she deserved love. Now, she had a divine identity and purpose.

In all my missionary experiences on and off my mission, even to this day, I've never seen a greater change in someone, a sweeter awakening, a deeper joy from knowing the divinity within and where it came from.

Hope fed her belief, her faith, her perspective, and her power. She walked away from the man that was paying her bills, even though she had no idea where the money would come from. "I deserve better," she told me. "I want more." She had hoped it. And now she believed it and acted on it.

It. Was. Astonishing.

She'd made amends with her family, and they were helping with the girls while Linda could work a second part time job to pay the rent.

By the time she'd set a baptismal date, Linda was a new person. She'd already felt reborn. She glowed with joy, peace, and love. This is the power of hope.

Sufficient Hope

Tucked into the latter part of the Book of Mormon is the record of a sermon preached by Mormon. I think it's safe to say that Mormon had seen some things in his life. He watched his people tragically kill and be killed physically and spiritually.

Still, against the odds, Mormon had a testimony of the power hope. Even in the midst of violence among his people and their mass exodus from the faith, Mormon, along with a few others, retained *"a sufficient hope by which [they] can enter into the rest of the Lord,* from this time henceforth until [they] shall rest with him in heaven."[32] And what did they hope for? It was "hope that through the atonement of Christ and the power of his resurrection, [that they would] be raised unto life eternal."[33]

---

32   Moroni 7:3 italics added.
33   Moroni 7:41.

Hope comes in many strengths and sizes. Linda's hope was young and fragile. Mormon's hope was lifelong and strong. But both had sufficient hope. Linda's hope carried her toward love and change. Mormon's hope solidified his faith and commitment.

Elder Dieter F. Uchtdorf describes hope

> like a beam of sunlight rising up and above the horizon of our present circumstances. It pierces the darkness with a brilliant dawn. It encourages and inspires us to place our trust in the loving care of an eternal Heavenly Father, who has prepared a way for those who seek for eternal truth in a world of relativism, confusion, and of fear.[34]

This is what hope did for Linda. She dared to hope she was worth loving. And when she dared to hope it was true, this hope moved her toward the choice to believe it was true and gained momentum until she had the faith to act as if it was true. Linda's hope was new and fragile, but sufficient to connect her with belief and faith. It moved her toward deity.

Remember, our divine discontent is our longing for light. Regarding this quest for light, Elder Uchtdorf said,

> The perfect place to begin is exactly where you are right now. It doesn't matter how unqualified you may think you are or how far behind others you may feel. The very moment you begin to seek your Heavenly Father, in that moment, the hope of His light will begin to awaken, enliven, and ennoble your soul.[35]

It's that marvelous? Hope can awaken, enliven, and ennoble your soul? Yes, please!

Sufficient hope leads to the choice to believe what you hope for is true. Belief is the hinge that holds hope and faith together. It is the middle child of the trio, the cream in the Oreo. What we choose to believe gives us power, joy, and blessings from heaven. When Elizabeth met her cousin Mary, who was with child with the Savior of the world, she exclaimed, "Blessed is she that believed."[36] The Savior told Jairus

---

34   Dieter F. Uchtdorf, *Pride and the Priesthood,* General Conference (Salt Lake City: The Church of Jesus Christ of Latter-day Saints), October 2010, Gospel Library App.

35   Dieter F. Uctdorf, *The Hope of God's Light,* General Conference (Salt Lake City: The Church of Jesus Christ of Latter-day Saints), April 2013, Gospel Library App.

36   Luke 1:45.

before He raised his daughter from the dead, "Be not afraid, only believe."[37] There is power in belief, and it starts with hope.

Many Hopes

Recently, in our Relief Society class, our teacher led a wonderful discussion on the topic of testimony. As we discussed our testimonies and how to strengthen them, one good sister in the back raised her hand. "I have many testimonies," she said. Then she proceeded to share with us the different things she had a testimony of: Jesus Christ, the gospel, prophets, etc. She said some of her testimonies are stronger than others, but she does what she can to nourish each one. It wasn't a novel concept, that our testimony of different things may not be the same, but I love the way she said it. "I have *many* testimonies."

I wonder if hope is like that. Though having hope in the perfect brightness of Jesus Christ is key, I think we can have many righteous complementary hopes. Hope that God really does know us, that He hears us, and that He loves us. Hope that He watches over our kids. Hope that the Atonement is real. Hope that the plan of happiness is real. Hope that we can change. Hope that we deserve to change. There are more things we can hope for than can be contained in this book. Indeed, we have many, many hopes.

I look back in my life and see countless times I hoped deeply. Sometimes my hope was born of fear of a negative outcome. When I sent my son on his mission, I hoped he'd be safe. When my daughter met a young man, I hoped she wouldn't get hurt. When I practiced my basketball skills for the ward women's basketball team, I hoped I wouldn't look stupid. I had hope, but my hope was to avoid the realization of my fears.

Other times my hope was out of desire for a positive outcome. We adopted our youngest when she was seven. I hoped she would love our family and we would love her. When I submitted a manuscript, I hoped it would get accepted. When I hinted to my husband a dozen times I wanted new kitchen knives for Christmas, I hoped he'd get them for me.

---

37   Mark 5:36.

But the kind of hope Linda had, and the kind of hope Mormon spoke about wasn't a hope of fear or preference, but the kind of divine hope that allows you to rest in the Lord. The kind of hope that casts its eyes toward heaven. It's the hope that these things we are taught—these glorious, magnificent, sometimes incomprehensible things—could actually be true.

Could we really be children of all-powerful Beings that created the universe? I hope so.

Is there more to life than what we can see? I hope so.

Can we really find purpose in our pain? I hope so.

Are we truly never alone? I very much hope so.

Take a moment and ask yourself what you hope for. What do you hope to have? What do you hope is truly real?

Sometimes it's hard to jump right to hoping the ultimate hope—that Jesus Christ came to save us because we are worth saving. And that's okay. Linda couldn't hope for this at the beginning. That hope was too big, and she felt too small. So, she first hoped there might be a chance that she could possibly be happy even if she didn't deserve it. That hope led her to hope that she could/would/did deserve happiness. She began to hope for love, for change, for purpose. Each hope moved her toward a choice to believe in that hope. Then, when she did, a new hope emerged.

This is one of the miracles of divine hope—it is evolutionary. Transformative. Hope builds upon hope. Each of our many hopes can move us toward faith and support the hope that trumps all hope, the hope in our Savior, Jesus Christ.

A Perfect Brightness

I have this fantastic neighbor who lives five houses up the street. She has a talent for making food that has blessed my heart and my hips many times. Over the years, we've traded recipes, cookies, bread, and ingredients. We joke that we are each other's local mercantile. At least monthly she or I will ask the other if we have eggs, brown sugar, butter, and the like. The text conversation is often like this:

-Hi Stephanie. Do you have happen to have one egg? I'm making cookies and I don't enough.
-I do! I'll send a kid over with it.
-You are *the* best!
-I know.

I can't tell you how many times she has saved my bacon, and even given me literal bacon, over the years. Without her help, I wouldn't have had what I needed in the moment I needed it.

I love how Paul describes God as "the God of hope."[38] His letter to the believing Romans was a powerful plea for them to hold on to the faith in a nation where believers were not only a minority, but often a persecuted minority. They had their struggles and questions, and the answer for Paul was always Jesus. Always. That is where he found his hope and strength. He chose to feed the hope God had given him, and he wanted the Roman saints to do the same. "Now," Paul continued, let "the God of hope fill you with all joy and peace in believing, that ye may abound in hope, through the power of the Holy Ghost."[39]

Let the God of hope fill you.

What a powerful plea.

Sometimes we are short on hope. We have things we want to believe in, faith we want to act on, but our hope might be missing. What can we do in the moments we lack hope? We can ask the God of hope who is near.

"Hi Father. Do you happen to have some hope? I'm facing a huge challenge right now and I don't think I have enough."

"I do! I'll send my Son over with it."

"You are *the* best!"

"I know."

This is the ultimate hope—hope in Jesus Christ. All our many divine hopes point us to Him, the One we hope will hear us, lead us, change us, save us, love us. Nephi calls this hope in Jesus Christ a "perfect brightness of hope."[40] There is power in our hope in Jesus Christ. President M. Russell Ballard said,

---

38   Romans 15:13.
39   Ibid.
40   2 Nephi 31:20.

I speak of hope in Christ not as wishful thinking. Instead, I speak of hope as an expectation that will be realized. Such hope is essential to overcoming adversity, fostering spiritual resilience and strength, and coming to know that we are loved by our Eternal Father and that we are His children, who belong to His family. When we have hope in Christ, we come to know that as we need to make and keep sacred covenants, our fondest desires and dreams can be fulfilled through Him.[41]

Remember Mormon's plea? That his people retain "a sufficient hope by which [they] can enter into the rest of the Lord, from this time henceforth until [they] shall rest with him in heaven."[42] Mormon simplifies this even further in his same sermon when he said, "And what is it that ye shall hope for? Behold, I say unto you that ye shall have hope through the atonement of Christ."[43]

Our youngest daughter, Grace, was seven when we adopted her. She didn't come from a religious background and so the concept of Jesus—though she'd heard His name before—was a foreign one. Over the years, we taught and testified of Jesus Christ. She learned the lingo. She memorized the primary answers. And yet, there was still shadows of disbelief in her eyes.

As she grew older in years and in the gospel, she began to understand more about the Savior and His Atonement. Forgiveness for sins was an awesome concept to her. You do something wrong and because of Him, it can be like you never did it. This was a stress-reducing principle she easily accepted. But her struggle was deeper than actions. It was the shame of who she was—the girl that she feared wasn't worth saving. We went to hours of therapy, which helped. We talked for hours at home, which helped. But nothing touched the shame the way Jesus did. In her teen years, she began to understand on a more complex level what Jesus did for us, for her. In theory, it was moving, but in reality, it was sometimes hard for her to even hope for. Did He really do that for her? Was she really worth His sacrifice? Could she really change? Could He love her after her choices sent Him to the cross?

41   M. Russell Ballard, *Hope in Christ*, General Conference (Salt Lake City: The Church of Jesus Christ of Latter-day Saints), April 2021, Gospel Library App.

42   Moroni 7:3.

43   Moroni 7:41.

She wasn't quite ready to believe these just yet, but when she chose to hope the answer was yes, that's when she began to change. Hope loosened shame's grip on our daughter, Grace, and allowed her to begin to love herself. It was the hope in Jesus Christ and His mercy and grace that gave her hope for a healthy future, a happy family, a healthy her. This hope in her Savior was sufficient to move her, in moments, from shame to self-love to Savior-love. I have seen Jesus save my daughter, literally, and it was because of hope that she let Him.

Feeding Hope

"What you feed grows." I first heard the phrase from the wife of my mission president in 1992, and I've repeated it a hundred times since. It's so true.

Hope isn't always easy to choose. It can be scary to hope. Just as Grace didn't want to be wrong, neither did Linda. What if Linda was being foolish? What if she was wrong? Linda was afraid of getting hurt again. The life she saw and lived didn't provide any proof that what she wanted to hope for was even possible. But she gave it a chance and it began to grow into belief then faith.

But here's the thing about hope. It is alive—a living thing. When it's nourished, given a chance, it can expand and become something more. But, when it's ignored or abused, it can fade and even die.

I wish I could tell you that Linda is in a wonderful place like Grace is right now. I wish I could tell you she went on to get baptized, that she met a wonderful man who saw her the way she saw herself and married her. I wish I could tell you there was a happy ending to this story. But I can't.

A week after we set her baptismal date, Linda disappeared. She stopped taking calls from the missionaries and from me. When I saw her in the parking lot, she hopped in her car before I could even say hi. Finally, after I'd stopped by a few times, she opened the door. She looked different. Grey. Sad. I asked her what was going on. She wasn't going to get baptized, she said. Her expression was cold as she told me she'd found out she was pregnant by the man that had been providing for her. She had stopped taking her medication, quit her evening job, and went back to him.

Her circumstance made me sad. But it's what she said next that broke my heart. "I didn't deserve it anyway," she said.

"Deserve what?" I asked.

"Happiness. A good life. God's love. It was stupid of me to think I did."

This was not the same Linda who was bright with hope just weeks before. That light in her eyes was gone. It seemed a part of her was gone.

Hope was gone.

She never spoke to me again. She avoided me, and, after I tried numerous times to talk to her, she finally told me to leave her alone. She moved when her lease was up. I have no idea where she is today. I am sad for that time in her life. But I'm still hopeful because that wasn't her ending. God knows her, and I am sure He has put other people in her life that can offer her hope. Of that, I have no doubt. But, on that day, she let go of hope. It broke my heart and hers.

I can hear what you're saying. This is supposed to be an inspiring chapter on hope, and yet, this story is sad. And you're right on both accounts. Hope is inspiring, and the ending to that part of her story is depressing, even tragic. But the cautionary lesson is powerful and critical to understand—hope floats until we shoot it down.

Satan knows if he can take away our hope, he can destroy our belief, our faith, our joy, and maybe even our love. He knows that, as Elder Jeffrey R. Holland has said, "our most indispensable virtues will be this precious gift of hope linked inextricably to our faith in God and our charity to others."[44]

Elder Holland goes on to say that "truly when hope is gone, what we have left is the flame of the inferno raging on every side." Hope is the target, and the adversary has a quiver of arrows on his back. If he can kill our hope, he can kill our belief and faith. If he can kill our hope, he can kill us, figuratively and literally.

---

44   Jeffrey R. Holland, *A Perfect Brightness of Hope*, General Conference (Salt Lake City: The Church of Jesus Christ of Latter-day Saints), April 2020, Gospel Library App.

I've seen the pain that comes when hope is starved. But I've seen the beauty that comes when it's fed. My daughter Grace loves herself now. When I asked her why she loves herself, she said it's because she knows she's a daughter of God, and He and Jesus love her. I love that she dared to hope in Jesus in challenging moments. I love that she fed her hope, even when it was hard.

How is our hope right now? Is it bright or brittle? For those of you with a bounty of hope, I say, keep feeding it. And to those who might have felt or are feeling hopeless right now, hear me when I tell you, hope is resilient. Grace's hope wasn't constant. She had many moments, even days, when she didn't have many hopes. Even times when she didn't have any. I, too, have had moments where I lost my grip on hope. It's a scary place, even if it's just for a moment. The adversary would have you stay there, in that desperate place. He would have you think hope is lost, that you are weak and perhaps even a broken or bad person if you have hopeless moments. But the Lord knows better.

I echo the powerful words of Sister Chieko N. Okazaki:

> Oh sisters, dearest sisters, choose life even though the forces of death seem strong! Choose hope even though despair seems close! Choose to grow even though circumstances oppress you! Choose to learn even though you must struggle against your own ignorance and that of others! Choose to love, even though ours are days of violence and vengeance. Choose to forgive, to pray, to bless another's life with simple kindness. Choose to build the sisterhood of the Relief Society by lifting and strengthening one another with love, testimony, faith, and service. I promise that you will feel the abundant love of the Savior. He receives each act of mercy to one of the least as one done to Himself. And in return He defies hopelessness, weariness, despair, and meaninglessness on our behalf.[45]

One of the many other things I love about hope is that it can spring up anywhere, even in dry ground. It's the resilience of hope—the hope of hope. If you've lost hope, even for a moment, that moment will be dark, for life without hope is dark. But it only takes the next moment

45   Chieko N. Okazaki, *Raised in Hope*, General Conference (Salt Lake City: The Church of Jesus Christ of Latter-day Saints), October 1996, Gospel Library App.

to choose hope again. Hope is never lost forever and sufficient hope is always a moment away.

Luckily—though it isn't luck—we all have Someone on our side that loves hope more than Satan hates it, Someone who is more powerful, more optimistic, more filled with hope and willing to give it. We have Jesus Christ. He wants us to accept hope, to abound in it, and to allow it to grow until it becomes "a perfect brightness of hope."[46] And we can.

Feed hope and it will grow. It's that simple. It may not be easy all the time, but it's simple. Here are a few ways you can feed your hope today:

- Let hope feed hope. Elder Uchtdorf said, "Each time a hope is fulfilled, it creates confidence and leads to greater hope."[47]
- Pray and ask God for the gift of hope.[48]
- The light of truth feeds hope. Gather light however you can, through scriptures, church, temple worship, service, study, and more.
- See the strength in vulnerability. Choosing and feeding hope can open us to feeling vulnerable. And that's okay. It might feel scary to say something like, "I hope I am worthy of love," because you might be afraid you're not. Being vulnerable means you allow risk, but it also allows the sweet, divine confirmation of our hope.
- Choose to hope even when everything around you seems hopeless. This is what Paul tried to teach the Romans when he said that blessed are those that "against hope believe in hope."[49]
- Seek for the whisperings of the Spirit.
- Enter in and strengthen your covenant relationship with God.
- Place your hope in Jesus Christ, your Savior and your friend.

I have loved pondering sufficient hope. It has changed the way I see and do many things. One of them is the way I pray. The other day, as I

---

46   2 Nephi 31:20.
47   Dieter f. Uctdorf, *The Infinite Power of Hope*, General Conference (Salt Lake City: The Church of Jesus Christ of Latter-day Saints), October 2008, Gospel Library App.
48   See Moroni 8:26.
49   Romans 4:18.

prayed, I took an inventory of what I hoped for with God. It was tender experience. So often, my prayers are filled with pleas for help, admissions of doubt, and apologies for being me. But, during this prayer, I looked into my mind and spirit, and shared with Heavenly Father what I truly hoped for for myself, my family, and others. I told Him I had hope that He is real, that He was listening. That I had hope that the gospel and the plan of happiness are real. And that I had hope that Jesus Christ is my Savior.

As I expressed my hope to my Father in Heaven, whisperings of the Spirit told me my many hopes were not in vain. What I hoped for was true. It was a tender and powerful experience, one that strengthened my hope, my belief, and my faith. My hope drew me closer to God and my Savior.

That is sufficient hope, my friends: tender, powerful, and effective.

Sufficient hope is ours to have if we choose it. So, let's choose it. Choose hope. Protect hope. Feed hope. Because sufficient hope is the spark that ignites the combustion engine of our belief. It is the gateway to all that is good and what leads to faith sufficient for miracles. It's what leads us to Jesus.

CHAPTER 4
Sufficient Faith

MY HUSBAND, JEREY, LOVES TO HIKE. THE MOUNTAINS FILL HIS SOUL. Warm homemade sourdough bread and writing the perfect sentence fill mine. But I do enjoy being out in nature, especially with Jerey.

A few years ago, Jerey wanted to take me on a hike up Fay Peak, a small peak in Mt. Rainier National Park. He said it would be "challenging but worth it." I was nervous. Those of you who know me are familiar with my hope/fear relationship with bears. I hope to see one in the wild but am also afraid it will look at me and see lunch. And there are a lot of bears here in the Pacific Northwest. I also wasn't sure if I could physically do it, but I hoped I could. And so, one unseasonably sunny October morning, we drove an hour through the foothills of Mt. Rainier to the Fay Peak trail head.

As we turned the corner toward the parking lot, I got my first peek at Fay Peak and instantly felt betrayed. This was not some benign hike through lush trees. No. Looming above us was a steep rock tower that rose 1500 feet to its peak. *This* was no hike. This was a mountain climb.

I wasn't sure I could do it. It was too tall. Too mountainy. It was simply too big. Jerey wisely made me a deal: take it step by step. One step at a time. That's all I needed to worry about—one step. And then, at any moment I feel I can't do it or I'm not enjoying myself anymore, we would turn around.

Without the pressure of having to make it to the top and with the promise I probably wouldn't be eaten by a bear, I double-knotted my hiking shoes, grabbed my walking sticks, said a prayer, and followed him up the path. One step at a time, I told myself. All I had to worry about was taking the next step.

The first part of the hike was beautiful. The elevation gain wasn't bad, and the scenery was breathtaking. Then, after an hour or so, the trail became steeper, winding up and toward the peak. I was challenged, but still willing to take the next step.

Soon, things started getting more difficult. My steps grew slower, closer together. I had to stop and catch my breath several times. The trail seemed less traveled. It was rocky and getting steeper by the foot.

Then, he told me it was time to scramble. And he wasn't talking about eggs. Scrambling, he explained, is when an incline is so steep that you need to use both your feet and hands to climb it. I did not see this part in the brochure.

I stood at the bottom of the steep section that looked more like a rock wall than part of a trail, and began to question my ability, desire, and my life's choices. This wasn't something I could do. I wasn't even sure if I wanted to do it.

I took a step back. Jerey reassured me we could turn around at any time. But, he said, if I could take just a few more steps, I would see something amazing.

Oh, I saw something amazing in my mind as I stood at the bottom of the 12-foot-high wall of jagged rock—a vision of me climbing halfway up and falling to my death. Or worse, falling and getting a bloody injury a bear would smell from across the forest like a shark in the water, find me, and eat me for an afternoon snack.

Still, I took a deep breath. *Just take the next step.*

I tucked my hiking sticks into my backpack and started up the rocky incline, using my hands and feet to pull me up the rocky section. I slipped but caught myself.

Take the next step.

Soon, I was near the top. I called down to Jerey to tell him I was almost there. He smiled and asked if I was ready. I took a deep breath and pulled myself up over the crowning rock to see what lay beyond my rock wall.

My breath stilled.

Green hills and deep valleys and towering mountain tops stretched before me for miles. I cannot express clearly enough the grandeur of the scene. It filled my mind with awe, my heart with joy, and my eyes with tears. In that moment, for the first time, I truly understood my husband's love affair with the mountains. They are a testimony of God and His creativity—and I could *feel* Him there.

What got me there? It wasn't my love of hiking or my determination to make it to the top. It started with an invitation which led to hope, which led to my choice to believe my husband, and my willingness to simply take the next step in faith. Each small act was sufficient to move me ahead.

There are thousands of words written over thousands of years about faith. Faith is wide and deep and complicated. It's power; it's belief; it's action. It can move mountains and still waters. But, the foundation of faith, this is what I want to focus on—the forward movement in the moment. The choice to believe what you hope for is true. It's hope and belief in action. It's purposeful forward movement, step by step, toward the grandeur of Lord.

Sufficient Faith

I love the account of the risen Savior visiting the people in the Americas. What it would be like to have been there? Soon after His glorious arrival, Jesus lets each person touch Him. He then gives the people His gospel and the ability to baptize in His name. He teaches them, calls twelve disciples, announces His fulfillment of the law of Moses, and speaks of the latter days.

It was a lot. And He knew it. In fact, He says to them: "I perceive that ye are weak, that ye cannot understand all the words which I am commanded of the Father to speak to you at this time."[50] He tells them to go home, ponder what they heard, and prepare to hear more the next day. And then He tells them He is going to leave.

---

50   3 Nephi 17:2.

But He doesn't.

What causes Jesus to change His mind?

It's their faith in Him.

Jesus sees the tears in their eyes and the pleas in their hearts and says, "I see your faith is sufficient that I should heal you."[51] And He does just that, healing each one that comes to Him, step by step.

There is so much I love about this account. But one thing I want to touch on is how it illustrates that faith and strength are not always synonymous. Remember, just a few verses before, Jesus sends them home because He perceives they are weak. And yet, even being weak in understanding, their faith is sufficient. Even in their weakness, their faith is all it needed to be to move them toward Jesus Christ, and in Him, they find their literal healing and their strength.

This is a brilliant Savior-centric moment. Oh I love this. *We can be weak and have faith at the same time.*

This truth brings me tremendous relief because honestly, I often feel weak. I often *am* weak. But my weakness—our weakness—does not preclude faith. This is what Paul meant when he said, "For when I am weak, then I am strong."[52] It's a beautiful truth that we will delve into more in Chapter 8.

Exercising sufficient faith isn't about being strong or fearless or doubtless. It's about active faith that propels us forward. We don't have to move mountains right now. We don't have to reach the summit. We don't have to know it all or have no doubts. We simply need to take the next step. This is sufficient faith—faith sufficient enough to move us one step closer to the Savior one moment at a time. And then, we take the next step, and the next.

I think of the small steps of the woman in the Bible who had an issue of blood. First, she heard about Jesus and went where He was. This faith brought her near Him. Then, step by step, she came even closer, close enough to touch His hem. I wonder if her heart and mind were racing. Was she nervous, afraid, overwhelmed? If she was, it didn't matter. Because she had sufficient faith to extend her arm and touch His clothes.

51   3 Nephi 17:8.
52   2 Corinthians 12:10.

A reach.

This is sufficient faith.

I think of Hannah praying for the millionth time for a child.

A plea.

This is sufficient faith.

I think of the woman who was a sinner, kneeling at Jesus's feet as she cleans them with her tears, dries them with her hair, and anoints them with oil.

A knee.

This is sufficient faith.

Sufficient faith is our hope, and in turn, belief, in action. Even in our weakness, our doubts, our fears, we can choose to let faith move us forward, however small that movement might be. We don't have to be a scripture expert, a gospel scholar, or even a person that is free of doubt or fear to have the faith sufficient for God. All that is required is a step, a reach, a plea, a knee. *Any* act of faith that directs us toward Him is sufficient in that moment. And He will meet us there, in our weakness, our sickness, our fears, our doubts, our anxiety, our grief, our sorrow, our pain.

This is the beauty of sufficient faith.

But what happens when our faith doesn't seem sufficient? What if our faith doesn't seem to work?

When Faith Doesn't Seem to Work

Faith is kind of a big deal. It's the foundational principle of the gospel.[53] It's the only way to salvation.[54] We can't do anything without faith.[55] It seems faith is an all-or-nothing principle. No wonder some people feel anxious when it comes to the subject of faith.

We hear miraculous stories of faith—how people are blessed because of their faith. I have my own story. During my pre-mission physical, my doctor found a lump in my breast. It concerned her enough that she scheduled an ultrasound the next day. I came home from that appointment with a mind full of thoughts and fears. I'd

53   Articles of Faith 1:4.
54   see Mosiah 3:12.
55   see D&C 8:10.

never faced the possibility of something serious in my health before. I'd never had to look at my mortality in that way before. I talked with my parents about it. We fasted and prayed together.

The next day, at the ultrasound, the technician was focused. Like, too focused. Typically, technicians aren't allowed to tell us what they see, but the concern on her face was too much for my comfort. So, I asked her if something was wrong.

"I can't find it," she said. "I can't find the lump. There isn't one." She searched with painful enthusiasm, but alas, never did find a lump to scan. She couldn't explain it. But I could. I was healed by my faith and the faith of my parents. It was a miracle. I was grateful, but not surprised because "true faith brings miracles, visions, dreams, healings, and all gifts of God that He gives to His Saints."[56] In my young mind, blessings were like a gumball machine. You stick a little faith in, turn the knob, and the blessing comes out.

I grew to understand that this concept, often called the "prosperity gospel," is not true.

Years later, my daughter, Paige, woke up on her second birthday terribly sick with the croup. While she was sick, she developed a rash which covered her little body. I took her to the doctor who told me that in response to her illness, Paige's body had developed eczema. Sometimes it goes away quickly on its own. But sometimes it doesn't. Paige's didn't.

For the next two years I watched eczema create raw patches of skin, raised itchy rashes, and areas of dry, broken lesions across her face and body. She looked more like a leper than a sweet toddler. It was hard not to see the expressions of people at the store, at church, or at school who pulled their children close to them, as if Paige was going to get them sick.

We tried everything we could think of to help her. We fed her whole foods. I made homemade pasta and bread. We went to doctors and specialists. We had all the creams, lotions, oatmeal baths. We filed her nails down so she wouldn't scratch herself raw during the day and

---

56   "Faith," Guide to the Scriptures (Salt Lake City: The Church of Jesus Christ of
      Latter-day Saints), Gospel Library App.

had to rubber band her sleeves over hands at bedtime so she wouldn't scratch in her sleep.

It was awful for her. Uncomfortable. Painful. And it was hard for me. I don't think there is anything more difficult than watching your children suffer.

One day, when Paige was four, she came into the house after playing in the back yard. The back of her t-shirt was covered in blood. Frantically, I checked underneath to find her back raw and torn up. I asked her what happened. She told me her back itched so badly she scratched it on the tree until she couldn't feel the itch anymore.

My heart broke.

I prayed and pleaded. She was an innocent child. She didn't deserve this. What more could I do to help her find relief?

Around that time, I remembered my pre-mission experience, and suddenly, I knew what to do. I needed to have more faith. I knew that God could heal her, and I knew that if my faith was strong enough, He would. That was the missing piece—my level of faith.

And so, I made a plan. I would request for a blessing of healing. To prepare, I prayed harder. I fasted more—all to show my complete faith in the Lord. I felt empowered. I was excited. My daughter was finally going to have relief. I'd seen miracles before that were born from my faith, and I knew—I *knew*—it would happen again.

The next morning, after the blessing, I snuck into Paige's room, excited to see my healed little girl. But she wasn't healed. She still had eczema. The next morning, she still had it. And the next morning. For the next 3,000 mornings, she would wake up with eczema, with the itchy skin, the sores, the scales. For the next 3,000 days she would get looks from people, have kids ask her if she was contagious. For the next 3,000 days she would be uncomfortable, in pain. And there was nothing I could do to make it go away.

I'll be honest. The months after my "faith plan" were hard for me. I asked a lot of questions: Did I not try hard enough? Did I not believe hard enough? Was my faith not strong enough? I blamed myself. If I had been stronger, better, had more faith, maybe Father would have healed her. It was my fault. The burden was heavy and painful.

Maybe you've felt this way some time in your life too, where you or your loved ones didn't seem to get relief no matter how hard you've tried. You might wonder if things would be different if you prayed more, had more faith, or done more. You might have done all you could and still saw no results and told yourself it was your fault. It is a heavy and painful place to be.

Once, I let my mind wonder if God really did care about Paige or me. Had He seen my sacrifices, my faith? Had He even heard my prayers all these years? Did He not see my faith in Him? Was He there? Was He even real?

It was a short moment. A blip. But, there, in that moment, I realized I had a choice to make. In the face of my faith and prayers not being answered the way I thought they would and should, I could choose to believe in God, or I could choose not to believe in Him.

I had the faith for Paige to be healed, but did I have the faith for her *not* to be healed?

Elder David A. Bednar laid a similar choice in front of a newly-wed couple when the husband was diagnosed with cancer. They asked Elder Bednar for a blessing. Before he gave them the blessing, they talked about their marriage and their trials. Then, Elder Bednar asked a question he hadn't planned on asking them, a question that had never occurred to Elder Bednar before.

> Do you have the faith not be healed? If it is the will of our Heavenly Father that you are transferred by death in your youth to the spirit world to continue your ministry, do you have the faith to submit to His will and not be healed?[57]

Can you imagine being asked that? I could. I asked myself nearly the same question. Did I have the faith not to have Paige be healed?

I learned a lot about faith through that experience. My faith brought me to God, to prayer, to fasting. But I realized afterward that I thought my faith would be proven by the results. It was my desire to get the outcome I wanted that drove my actions. I wasn't submitting my will to Him; I was submitting my plans to Him. Elder Bednar said that "strong faith in the Savior is submissively accepting of His will and

---

57   David A. Bednar, "Accepting the Lord's Will and Timing," *Ensign,* August 2016.

timing in our lives—even if the outcome is not what we hoped for or wanted."[58]

I don't know why God let Paige suffer for so long. But honestly, I've stopped asking why. Rather, I focus on *who*. I point my faith to God and Jesus Christ, trusting them, accepting Their timing and will. Nephi had his share of struggles. A refugee whose brothers tried to kill him, a man who did things he never thought he could do, a man who talked with the Lord face to face. I'm sure he had a lot of questions. But, in his words, "I know that [God] loveth his children; nevertheless, I do not know the meaning of all things."[59] I choose to love God. I choose to believe He loves me and wants what's best for me and for my daughter. I choose to trust Him. I accepted His will.

Another question I've stopped asking is, "Did my faith work?" As of this writing, she is twenty-five and though her eczema has subsided over the years, she still has uncomfortable spots and breakouts. If my faith was defined by God's submission to my pleas, then no, it would not seem it worked. However, the greatest truth I learned through this experience is that faith is not about getting what I want but wanting to accept God and what He has to give. My faith is defined now by my submission to God's will. It's defined by my efforts to come to Him, not His efforts to give me everything I ask for.

Seeing faith in this light can be hard. But we can do it. Even when life doesn't look like we want it to, we can come to understand that faith isn't about removing pain but inviting God and Jesus into the pain with us. We can choose to trust in Them and to trust Them. And when we do, we will find our eyes will be open to so many of the wonderful things They are already giving us, even in our pain and challenges.

As I look back at that time now, I can see the fruits of my faith. I can see how I was supported by God. I was led to certain doctors. I received inspiration on how to help ease her pain at home. I even figured out how to use my pasta making attachment on my Kitchen Aid. When I peel my focus away from what I didn't receive, I can see so many things I did.

58   Ibid.
59   1 Nephi 11:17.

The faith I had then didn't heal Paige. But, my faith, my choice to believe, was sufficient to propel me toward Heavenly Father and Jesus Christ, to feel Their power and Their love in my life, and to see it in Paige's life as well. They have been with her and with me this entire time, working other miracles outside and inside of us.

Sufficient faith works, my friends. Faith in God and in Jesus Christ works. Even if we don't always see the external reward for our faith, we can always count on the internal movement from our faith. It moves us toward Them, one prayer at a time, one plea at a time, one rejoicing at a time, one choice at time, one pause at a time, one step at a time. It's not about getting what we want but moving toward those who can give us what we need, even in the middle of suffering. This is the beauty of sufficient faith.

In the Moment

I am a visual learner. It's one of the reasons the mass transition to digital scriptures has been a challenge for me. I love how my scriptures feel, how they look. I struggle to remember exact references; I just know that my favorite verse about the Atonement is in the middle-ish of Alma in the lower left column of the right page. I also know the verses I love most are not only underlined in red and highlighted in yellow, but also have a single red heart placed by them. These are the "heart" verses that reach the very depths of my soul.

One of my "heart" verses is in Luke, in the upper left-hand column of a left page. It says, "Lord, increase our faith."[60] There have been many times in my life when I felt my faith wasn't strong enough, so I went to the Lord in prayer and begged Him to bless me with greater faith. This is why I marked it with a heart; it's one of my personal pleas.

And yet, as I come to a greater understanding of sufficient faith, I see a small error in my cry. No, the *reasoning* behind my cry. So often, when I have asked for an increase in faith, it was because I felt my faith wasn't where it *should* be—that my current faith wasn't enough.

But, enough for what? Usually, I asked God to increase my faith because I think I should be able to handle life better, doubt less,

---

60   Luke 17:5.

serve more—do and be better. This was my *enough* mentality shining through.

However, when we look at faith through the eyes of *sufficient* we don't need to be worried about having total faith, immovable faith, or the faith enough to overcome the trials ahead of us. If the size and strength of our faith is enough to move us toward Jesus Christ, in that moment, it is all it needs to be; it *is* sufficient.

This is yet another beauty of sufficient faith: it's about present faith, as in faith in this moment.

The man who brought his suffering son to Jesus for healing has sufficient faith, even if he doesn't think so. He begs Jesus to have compassion on them. Jesus replies, "If though canst believe, all things are possible to him that believeth."[61]

This man cries out, through tears, "Lord, I believe; help thou mine unbelief."[62]

Here is a father who was unsure of his belief, if his foundation of faith is enough. And yet, look where he is. Look *who* he is near. Whatever deficits exist in his perceived faith don't matter. The faith that he *does* have is what brings Him to the Savior.

I love Elder Holland's commentary on this short but powerful event:

> Observation number one regarding this account is that when facing the challenge of faith, the father asserts his strength first and only then acknowledges his limitation. His initial declaration is affirmative and without hesitation: "Lord, I believe." I would say to all who wish for more faith, remember this man! The size of your faith or the degree of your knowledge is not the issue—it is the integrity you demonstrate toward the faith you do have and the truth you already know.[63]

That last line is powerful. It is also a description of sufficient faith— it is *how* we act on what we have chosen to believe. Whatever we do in faith, big or small, *is* sufficient in that moment.

---

61   Mark 9:23.
62   Mark 9:24.
63   Jeffrey R. Holland, *Lord, I Believe*, General Conference (Salt Lake City: The Church of Jesus Christ of Latter-day Saints), April 2013, Gospel Library App.

After the father pleads for help with his unbelief, the Savior heals his son. Even with faith he doesn't feel is full enough, it is sufficient in that moment to bring him to the Lord who, in that moment, sees it is sufficient to heal.

The Lens of Sufficient Faith

When I was a young girl while visiting my Grandma Parker, she and I stood side by side as we washed the dinner dishes by hand. I grabbed a plate that was covered in dried food and scrubbed to no avail. Finally, my grandma gently put her hand on mine. "Watch," she said as she plugged the sink and filled it with hot water. Then she took the plate from me and placed it underwater. "Let the hot water do its work." After a few minutes, she pulled the plate out of the water and handed it me. The wet food wiped off easily.

To me, this is a wonderful example of sufficient faith. We put ourselves in Their care so They can do a marvelous work in and with us. We let Heavenly Father and the Savior do Their work.

The adversary would have us think our faith has to be noonday bright to be real faith. He wants us to look at faith through the self-centric view of *enough*, to think that faith is about us believing enough and doing enough to become like God. He wants us to think that having faith means *we* need to earn blessings, to try harder each day to qualify to return to Heaven. It puts the onus of perfection on us.

Those are all lies.

Only One can change us, perfect us, and save us: Jesus Christ. He wants us to have Savior-centric sufficient faith. He wants us to do what we need to do in the moment to move us in the direction of Him because *He* is the one who perfects us. He is the one who makes us whole. Sufficient faith is about letting Him do His work in us.

Exercising sufficient faith is not a one-size-fits-all. In fact, it will probably look different every day. Your sufficient faith today, in this moment, might look like praying for the first time in days. Next month it might be walking into the temple. Today it might look like letting go of a grudge. Next year it might look like walking through the chapel doors. Sufficient faith is about what we need in this moment to draw close to God and His Son, and that will look different at different times in our lives.

Exercising sufficient faith is not about doing more or less. It's about doing what He has asked us, for the right reason. It's about action and intent. It doesn't matter how big or small the act, if the intent is righteous. President Henry B. Eyring said that "with sufficient faith, we will ask for direction *with the intent* to go and do whatever He asks."[64] This probably looks a lot like what you are already doing now: praying, reading your scriptures, attending church, serving in the temple, and making and keeping your covenants. In the words of Elder W. Mark Bassett,

> As we strive to act righteously by making and keeping sacred covenants and applying the doctrine of Christ in our lives, our faith will not only be sufficient to carry us . . . but with the Lord's help we will also be capable of moving stones that are in our path.[65]

Back to my hike—I mean, my mountain climb. After I took in my triumphant breathtaking view, I looked up and realized I still wasn't at the top. I still had a way to go to reach the peak of Fay Peak. Because the path was steep and rocky, Jerey moved in front of me where I was able to follow him closely. I'll admit, this part was scary. We were above the trees, scrambling up exposed rock to a peak that looked too small for my comfort. I listened as he guided me, avoiding loose stones and unstable ground. I stepped where he stepped. I stayed close to him. And, eventually, together, we made it to the summit.

There, standing side by side, we could see for miles in every direction. Mt. Rainier loomed in front of me. I turned to see Mt. Baker off in the distance. And turned again to see Mt. St. Helens on the horizon. It was truly breathtaking. I was on top of the world, seeing things in a way I had never seen before. This wasn't just one slice of a glorious view, like I had when I reached the first peak; this was a 360-degree panorama of magnificence.

---

64   Henry B Eyring, *The Faith to Ask Then to Act*, General Conference (Salt Lake City: The Church of Jesus Christ of Latter-day Saints), October 2021, Gospel Library App.

65   Mark W. Bassett, *After the Fourth Day*, General Conference (Salt Lake City: The Church of Jesus Christ of Latter-day Saints), April 2023, Gospel Library App.

You can see the metaphor, can't you.

Heavenly Father has wonderful things in store for us—the exquisiteness of charity, the magnificence of forgiveness, the vastness of His grace, the immensity of His power. And He has given us a way, *the* way, to receive them through faith in Jesus Christ.

The real beauty of sufficient faith is that we don't have to follow the Savior to the top of a metaphorical mountain before we can experience these wonderful things. The moment we reach for Him is the moment He can heal us, strengthen us, teach us, guide us, bless us, change us, and help us move further along this path of eternal life, side by side, one beautiful sufficient step at a time.

And this is inspiring indeed.

CHAPTER 5

Sufficient Humility

I WAS VISITING WITH A SWEET SISTER ONE DAY DURING A MINISTERING interview. Our conversation wandered through the sisters she ministered to, to her life, to her doubts and her loves, and even to me. At the end of our visit, I asked her to close with a prayer. She prayed for her companion and her sisters, then she prayed for me, that I would have the capacity to do all the things I was being asked to do.

But then, she prayed for something that caught me completely by surprise. She said, "Please bless her to know where she is not needed."

In that moment, time seemed to slow as the doors of self-awareness opened and revealed the truth that I was overwhelmed. The days before her prayer were filled with obligations and opportunities. They were all good, and I wanted to do them all and gave a valiant effort.

The days after her sweet prayer were filled with self-analysis. Through study and prayer, I came to realize that my problem wasn't only overscheduling or obligation. It was a problem with pride. I was leaning on myself, not the Lord. I had taken it upon myself to do all the good things—necessary *and* extra—because . . . because why? Because I could? Because I felt I should? I mean, if I *can* do it, then I *should*, right?

And so, even with good intentions, I blazed forward in my own self-confidence and ability down a path of over scheduling and exhaustion.

Here is a truth I realized: if I had a problem with pride, then I had, at the same time, a problem with humility. I also realized I needed a better understanding of what humility was.

One thing I did and do know is humility is key to our happiness as we strive for eternal life. Elder Quentin L. Cook shared that humility is "essential to achieve the Lord's purpose for us."[66] (Cook, 2018). Alma, in his powerful sermon of self-evaluation and visualization, asked his people, "Could ye say, if ye were called to die at this time, within yourselves, that ye have been sufficiently humble?"[67] And Jesus Christ, Himself, speaks of humility as the key to seeing Him. He says, "inasmuch as you strip yourselves from jealousies and fears and humble yourselves before me . . . the veil shall be rent and you shall see me and know that I am."[68]

Though humility is crucial to our eternal purpose, oftentimes it can be misunderstood. In fact, sometimes thinking about humility can make some of us feel bad. We might feel guilt for the pride we struggle with or embarrassment or guilt for our weaknesses.

In fact, many of us—my past self included—feel that to be humble requires a level of self-loathing. I mean, King Benjamin reminds his people (and us) of their "nothingness" and implored them to "humble yourselves in the depths of humility."[69] Sometimes we feel that to be humble is to acknowledge we are broken, insignificant, incapable, nothing.

And so, in our quest to be humble, we end up on our knees each night apologizing. We feel bad for not just what we've done, but *who we are.* This is shame. And it's what can happen when we look at humility through the lens of enough.

I looked at humility through the lens of enough for much of my life. I made humility about what I was doing and being. I worked hard to see my weakness so God could make me strong like the scriptures taught[70] I apologized for the desire for approval from others and

---

66　　Quentin L. Cook, *The Eternal Everyday*, General Conference (Salt Lake City: The Church of Jesus Christ of Latter-day Saints), April 2017, Gospel Library App.

67　　Alma 5:27.

68　　D&C 67:10.

69　　Mosiah 4:11.

70　　see Ether 12:27.

repented for the satisfaction I allowed myself to feel when I accomplished something. I wanted so badly to do as the Apostle Peter taught, to humble myself under the mighty hand of God, that He may exalt me in due time.[71] I made humility about me.

The problem was, when I made humility about myself, the moment I admit I was humble, I thought I then introduced pride and was knocked down again. It was a never-ending cycle of trying to be but never being humble enough.

But, when we begin to see humility through the lens of sufficient, we move our focus from what we do and are to *what we can obtain.* We move our focus from a self-centric one to a Savior-centric one. We move away from trying to *be* humble and move toward an imperfect person who *has* humility.

This was the shift in my own perspective, helped by the prayer of that sweet sister.

Not too long after that experience, as I pondered what humility really was, I grabbed my laptop, got in my car, and drove to the temple. The following is my experience written in real-time:

I am sitting in my car behind the Seattle temple. The gold-etched words "The House of the Lord" and "Holiness to the Lord" are gleaming in the late afternoon sun.

I love the temple. The Lord's house. Our Father's house. This is where my spirit longs to be.

My husband heard someone call the temple "God's embassy on earth." This rings true. No matter what country you're in, the moment you walk through the embassy gates, you are on homeland. There are times when this world feels foreign to me. I love that I can come to a temple—any temple—and walk through the doors and be on heavenly homeland.

I've come today to worship God and receive revelation about humility, what it means, what it is.

The sun is shining. A slight breeze moves through my open windows. An older gentleman with a white shirt, tie, and sun hat is walking through the parking lot. Security. It makes me smile. A squirrel is

---

71   see 1 Peter 5:6.

running across the grass and now up a tree. A bird landed in the tree twenty feet from me just now and is watching me. And I can feel God near. Even before I enter the doors, I feel the holiness of this place.

It makes me feel good. Safe. It reminds me of who I am to God and my Savior and who They are to me. It reminds me of how much I need them—totally and so completely. And how deeply I am grateful for Them.

Just now, I scanned the pile of notes I've been collecting on humility and stopped at the definition I pulled from the Church's Gospel Topics page a few days ago: "To be humble is to recognize gratefully our dependence on the Lord—to understand that we have constant need for His support. Humility is the acknowledgment that our talents and abilities are gifts from God. It is not a sign of weakness, timidity, or fear; it is an indication that we know where our true strength lies . . . [Jesus] always acknowledged that His strength came because of His dependence on His Father" (Gospel Topics - Humility, 2023).

And suddenly, in this moment, it makes sense to me, this understanding and revelation that is happening in real time. What I am feeling is humility. *It is a sweet feeling, a tender thing. It is seeing myself and my Father and Brother clearly. And it feels like home.*

This experience solidified the way I look at humility. The way I feel about humility. And the way I *feel* humility in my soul. It reminded me that I've had humility before, that I've known what it is and how good it feels.

One of my favorite words is *perspective*. My first book, *Does This Insecurity Make Me Look Fat?* is not a body-image or weight loss book, but one focused completely on perspective and the courage, strength, and joy that comes when we see ourselves, others, life, and God through His eyes.

Perspective is where we look and how we choose to see. It's also key in having humility. When we have pride, we are focused on ourselves in relation to others and even in relation to our own expectations (the *enough* lens). But when we shift to real humility, our focus is on God.

C. S. Lewis speaks of this shift of vision when he said,

In God you come against something which is in every respect immeasurably superior to yourself . . . as long as you are proud you cannot know God. A proud man is always looking down on things and people: and, of course, as long as you are looking down, you cannot see something that is above you.[72]

Humility isn't about looking at ourselves and loathing. It's not about trying to do and be everything while avoiding credit. It's about looking to God and seeing Him. When we see Him, we see ourselves in thankful clarity. We realize how much He loves us and has done for us. We are teachable. We trust Him and accept His timing. We recognize how magnificent He thinks we are. We see and receive the gifts He wants to give us and magnify them with joy. And we see ourselves as He does—not broken, dirty, failing mortals, but toddler gods and goddesses who are reaching for Him as we stumble His way.

Humility is about moving our eyes and souls toward Him, connecting with Him, and feeling home.

The Enemies of Humility

As in anything that is good, humility has its share of enemies.

The first enemy isn't really an enemy. But the effect can still be detrimental. It is the mistake we make by looking at only a few parts of the humble family rather focusing on the whole.

Bear with me for a second while we get some linguistic logistics out of the way to understand the humble family. (My freshman English teacher, Cecil Ringgenberg, who loved words, would be so proud.) The humble family consists of three parts:

1. Humility (noun): The clear perspective of who God is and who we are, accompanied by gratitude and love.
2. Humble (adjective): The word that describes someone with humility.
3. Humble (verb): The process, either inwardly chosen or outwardly compelled, by which we gain humility, or become humble.

72   C. S. Lewis, *Mere Christianity*, New York: HarperOne, 2001.

This family is important. In the scriptures, we are told to be humble;[73] we are counseled to humble ourselves and warned we might be humbled;[74] and we are instructed to have humility.[75] Having humility, being humble, or being humbled are beautifully linked together to bring us to a state of pure perspective, love, and wonder.

Part of the struggle many of us have had or still have is that we focus intently on the last two, the adjective and verb. We have good intentions. I know we do. And these are wonderful things to work on! But problems arise when we stop there. We can get stuck in the *enough* lens as we (sometimes clumsily) try to humble ourselves or strive to *be* humble and not move beyond. When we don't lift our eyes past these two very good things, we make it about ourselves, our performance, and our perfection. *We* have to *be* humble.

Not focusing on the entire family of humility can be one of the culprits of negative feelings. When we make humility about ourselves, there is little to no room for success. When *becoming* humble is the goal, the moment we finally admit we *are* humble is the same moment we tell ourselves we've just failed at being humble. Ironically, being humble becomes the goal we can never check the beloved box for. Frustration and even hopelessness set in as our effort to *be* humble becomes yet another piece of evidence of our performance failure.

When we view humility through the lens of sufficient, we stretch our vision and goal beyond ourselves to God. Being humbled and being humble aren't, then, the end goals, but the vehicle and byproduct of the ultimate goal—to gain humility so we can see God and ourselves clearly.

To clarify the difference, Elder Cook explained that

> humility isn't some grand identifiable achievement or even overcoming some major challenge . . . It is *having* the quiet confidence that day by day and hour by hour we can rely on the Lord, serve Him, and achieve His purposes.[76]

---

73   see Alma 7:23.
74   see Alma 32:16.
75   see D&C 107:79.
76   Quentin L. Cook, *The Eternal Everyday*, General Conference (Salt Lake City: The Church of Jesus Christ of Latter-day Saints), April 2017, Gospel Library App.

Another enemy of humility is pride. Remember this C. S. Lewis's quote? "A proud man is always looking down on things and people: and, of course, as long as you are looking down, you cannot see something that is above you."[77]

Pride keeps our focus on ourselves—specifically how we look compared to others and our own expectations. Pride keeps our eyes down and sideways rather than up.

I know pride well. She is an old friend of mine who shows up too often and usually during the most inopportune times.

For example, I've done a lot of speaking in my time. Typically, I don't get nervous. In fact, after I have prepared well, I am one of those peculiar ones who love to teach and speak about the gospel to groups large and small.

A few years ago, while I was serving as Stake Relief Society president, I was asked to speak in the adult session of Stake Conference. I was happy to accept. I had done it before and felt confident in my ability to give a good talk.

I was given the topic of welfare—a broad and beautiful topic with a thousand directions I could go. The visiting general authority asked that I and the other speakers not write our talks, but prepare and speak by the Spirit. This wouldn't be a problem for me as I hadn't written a talk in years. I had grown accustomed to using bullet points and sometimes no notes at all when I spoke. And so, I prepared with confidence and enthusiasm.

Normally, as I have prepared talks or presentations, I feel a bit restless until all the pieces fall into place. I know that I have prepared the right message in the right way when peace overcomes me. And it happens every time.

But it didn't happen this time.

I had spent hours studying. I poured through conference talks, scriptures, and stories as I searched for the right angle I should take. I wanted to give a good talk. I'd be extra pleased if it were entertaining and compelling. I mean, I *am* a speaker, so there was an expectation, right? But that feeling of peace never came. I just couldn't seem to pin

---

77   C. S. Lewis, *Mere Christianity*, New York: HarperOne, 2001.

down what I should say. I had searched and studied welfare until the moment I had to leave for the meeting.

The day of the conference arrived. Per tradition, when a general authority comes, the stake Relief Society presidency prepares and serves dinner to the stake presidency, their wives, and our special guests prior to the adult session. I stole quiet moments during our dinner prep to go over what I'd studied. Despite my faithful efforts, I still had no idea what I was going to say.

With fifteen minutes until the meeting started, I tucked myself into an empty classroom and prayed. *Please help me to know what to say. Please help me to be a good speaker. Please help me not to look stupid. Please help me say things that will help those who have come. Please, just help me.*

Still, nothing.

And then it occurred to me—this is one of those situations you read about where God tests your faith. That was it! I had put the work in. Now, all I had to do was have faith. I was a good speaker. I just had to stand at the microphone and do my thing. He'd take care of me and tell me what to say. Relief washed over me. This was a test, and I had the faith to pass it.

I confidently took my seat next to the general authority. The meeting started. I still didn't know what I was going to say, but I knew it would be good. I was prepared and capable, and God would make it so. The stake president spoke. I prayed. Another speaker or two spoke. I prayed. And then, it was my turn.

I walked up to the pulpit and stood, just three feet in front of the general authority, facing the sea of stake members. I smiled, waiting for the words to come, words that would be eloquent and profound. But nothing came.

I blinked.

I prayed again, but my mind was blank.

The following eight minutes were a painful blur. I stumbled over my words as I tried to create a patchwork of welfare bits and pieces. I was sweating. I was forgetting. I was stammering. I was a mess.

I sat down and the general authority, bless his heart, leaned over and whispered, "That was a lovely talk."

I fought back tears because I knew it wasn't. I could do better than that. I mean, I had done better than that so many times before. I *was* better than that. And I had to sit there for another hour in front of hundreds of people who knew it too.

After the meeting, I held the tears at bay while my presidency and I cleaned up the dinner dishes and the kitchen. On the way out to my car, I ran into a good friend who complimented my talk. I gave her a challenging look and told her to be honest. "Well," she said apologetically, "it wasn't your best." I knew she was right.

The moment I closed the door of my car, I began to cry. The tears I'd held back flowed freely and loudly. I was embarrassed. I was confused. And I was hurt.

I prayed again. *I'm sorry I failed. I'm so dumb. But why didn't you tell me what to say? Why did you abandon me? Where were you?*

Then Heavenly Father, in His typical way, gave me an answer I wasn't expecting. There, sitting in my car, I realized that this was a lesson on humility. I understood that I hadn't come to Heavenly Father for help in writing the talk *He* had wanted to me to give. Rather, I had been focused on *me* giving a good talk, on *me* impressing others, on *me* living up to the expectation that I was a good speaker. Even with intentions I thought were good—giving a good talk—the drive behind it was self-centric. I had let my pride make it about *me*.

I love these words of Elder Gary E. Stevenson:

> Pride is the opposite of humility . . . When prideful, we tend to honor ourselves rather than giving it to others, including the Lord. Pride is often competitive; it is a tendency to seek to obtain more and presume we are better than others. Pride often results in feelings of anger and hatred; it causes one to hold grudges or to withhold forgiveness. Pride, however, can be swallowed in the Christlike attribute of humility.[78]

I could fill this book with the enemies of humility, but I wanted to focus on the one that I think is the most insidious. That enemy is shame.

Elder Stevenson and many, many others have said that pride is the opposite of humility. I propose that shame is too. Pride keeps us from

---

78   Gary E. Stevenson, *Spiritual Eclipse,* General Conference (Salt Lake City: The Church of Jesus Christ of Latter-day Saints), October 2017, Gospel Library App.

God because we feel we don't need Him and all He has to give. Shame, however, keeps us from God because we feel we don't deserve Him and all He has to give.

The adversary loves shame. He will use anything he can to make us hate ourselves. Even the misinterpretation of humility. Elder Uchtdorf refuted Satan's tactic powerfully when he said:

> Some suppose that humility is about beating ourselves up. Humility does not mean convincing ourselves that we are worthless, meaningless, or of little value. Nor does it mean denying or withholding the talents God has given us. We don't discover humility by thinking less *of* ourselves; we discover humility by thinking less *about* ourselves."[79]

Shame keeps us from making eye contact with God. But He is exactly who we should be looking at—who we deserve to see and be seen by. Humility isn't averting our eyes away from God because of who we think we are or aren't, but locking our eyes on Him because of who He is.

If reading this pinches at your soul, if you're hearing whispers that maybe I'm wrong because I don't know what you've done or who you are, or if you're reminding yourself that God knows who you are and what you've done (or have had done to you) and doesn't feel you're worthy—you are feeling shame, my friend.

Brené Brown, a dedicated researcher of shame, said of the thousands of people she interviewed,

> there was only one variable that separated the people who have a strong sense of love and belonging and the people who really struggle for it. And that was, the people who have a strong sense of love and belonging believe they're worthy of love and belonging. That's it. They believe they're worthy.[80]

I want to tell you right now, you are worthy. Who you are—the very core of your soul—is divine. God loves you and wants to connect with you. He wants you to connect with Him, and shame is standing

79   Uchtdorf, *Pride and the Priesthood*, General Conference, (Salt Lake City: the Church of Jesus Christ of Latter-day Saints), October 2010, Gospel Library App.

80   Brené Brown, *The Power of Vulnerability*, TED Talks, June 2010, Accessed February 28, 2024, www.ted.com/talks/brene_brown_on_vulnerability.

in your way. Striving to have humility is key. There, with humility in your head and heart, you can see God as He is—kind and loving—and see yourself as you are—His child who is worth loving, worth forgiving, worth blessing, and worth living.

Sufficient Humility

Now that we know what humility is and what it isn't, the question is, what is sufficient humility? The short answer is humility draws our eyes and souls toward Heavenly Father and Jesus Christ. Like sufficient hope and faith, sufficient humility is about *having* what we need in the moment to connect us to Heaven.

I am grateful that salvation is won in moments. There are some moments, hours, or days, where I feel I have humility sufficient to keep me aligned with God. And then, as I mentioned before with my epic fail of a talk, there are times when I choose to cling onto my own talents and skills rather than humility.

It's hard, at least for me, to consistently have humility. Having humility brings me strength, perspective, and power. I wish it stayed with me always. But I am imperfect and the enemies of humility are strong. To me, humility often feels like a helium balloon I am continually reaching for and pulling toward me. The moment I ease my grip, it begins to float away. I wonder if this is what "enduring to the end" really is—a continual effort to hold onto the things that bring us closer to Jesus Christ.

The Jaredites have a lot of experience with this. Over thousands of years, they move in and out of humility. At times they move themselves back into view. Other times, God gave them a nudge.

We find one such nudge in Ether chapter nine. The Jaredites experience years of strife and contention which is followed by a time of peace and prosperity. And then, as so often happens, they side-step away from humility and over to pride and disbelief. Prophets are sent to warn them with the hope they would reconnect with God. But the people reject them.

Then, a drought hits. And it hits hard. People die from starvation. They are chased out of their lands by poisonous snakes and then blocked from returning home. They are dying and desperate. It sounds awful, doesn't it? I will take struggling at the pulpit over starving by the wayside any time. But God knows what it takes to move them back to Him. For the Jaredites, it takes desperation.

In this desperation "they began to repent of their iniquities and cry unto the Lord."[81] They begin to move back toward God. "And it came to pass that when they had humbled themselves sufficiently before the Lord he did send rain upon the face of the earth; and the people began to revive again."[82]

I love the image of these hurt and hungry people inching themselves toward God, prayer by prayer. And when they inch themselves sufficiently, they find themselves connected with God. They find humility.

They aren't perfect, nor are they perfectly humble. And that's okay. The Lord isn't expecting perfection during this life. They do, however, make the choice to do what they needed to do to *have* the humility sufficient to be blessed. "And then the Lord did show forth his power unto them in preserving them from the famine."[83]

The Lord's intent wasn't for them to feel terrible about themselves, but for them to feel good about Him, to *see* Him. To be close to Him. This opened the door for the Lord to bless them.

As with sufficient hope and faith, sufficient humility doesn't require perfect humility. If our humility effectively moves us closer to light, to truth, to change, to Him and all that He has to give us in this moment, it is sufficient.

The Resilience of Humility

Humility allows us to view God in a clear light, to see ourselves with kind eyes, and look at life with greater confidence. Each of these things are beautiful.

But I think one of the most beautiful, and perhaps powerful, fruits of humility is resilience. We can find this resilience in another one of my favorite words: *nevertheless.*

---

81   Ether 9:34.
82   Ether 9:35.
83   Ibid.

The Savior had perfect humility. In all the records we have of His life, He was only and always about His Father's will. He never asked for anything different. Except once.

As the heaviness of the Atonement settled in, Jesus prayed in the Garden of Gethsemane: "Father, if thou be willing, remove this cup from me: *nevertheless* not my will, but thine, be done."[84]

I believe Jesus knew it had to happen, that it would happen, because He chose to allow it to happen. But, in that moment, it seems He didn't want it to happen. He saw His Father clearly. He saw Himself clearly. He saw us clearly. He saw love clearly. This humility gave Him the strength to walk into the most painful experience of His life.

The resilience of humility can help us in our lives as we sometimes walk into hard places. Places where loss, grief, fear, and doubts may reside. Humility—even humility in just a small moment—can give us the perspective and power to continue, to live life each day as it ebbs and flows between joy and pain, the extraordinary and the mundane. Humility can ground us, rooting us deeply in our identity and purpose. This resilience was beautifully expressed by my grandmother, Jane Steed in her poem, "Trees in an Autumn Storm."

May I bow before God, as do the trees
Before the culling autumn storms—
gracefully, never fighting winds not seen.
Upper branches filled with new growth,
Responding to the sometimes thrashing torrents of rain.
For them, no hiding place from God's time-to-time testing.
They are out in the open; vulnerable, accepting,
Lifting from the roots skyward, stretching toward heaven.
And when the storms come, as they always do,
They appear to accept and even enjoy their time of challenge.
Roots reaching deep hold base trunk secure, firm, sure.
The bending to the winds will come from the reaching latter growth.
That which has not before experienced the storm
will stand or fall from the nurturing trunk
As heavenly forces call for an accounting of new growth.

---

84   Luke 22:42, italics added.

Thrashing, swaying, twisting, accepting, ever accepting
'Till the storm is through.
Then, all becomes calm, as gentle rain descends,
Bathing each leaf and branch with healing touch.
The trial is over. The sky lightens.
The trees stretch once again heavenward.
Upon the ground lie twigs and leaves, and sometimes branches
that stood well when there was no storm.
Weaknesses hiding amid the strengths, 'till now.
The trees do not mourn the loss.
They have been pruned by the God that created them.
That which was strong has become stronger.
They are filling the measure of their creation.
There are lessons to be learned from autumn's storms—
About life, and God, and growth, and obedience,
And so many other things—
If we could just open our eye and hearts
To the simple, visual parable of trees in an autumn storm.

Sufficient humility isn't about being good enough for God. It's not about being perfect or self-abasing. It's about connecting with Him, moment to moment. And in those moments of sufficient humility, we find strength, growth, joy, and love. We find God. And we find ourselves.

Even if, a moment ago, you were pulled down by guilt or shame. Now, in *this* moment—in any moment—you can turn your eyes, your heart, your will to God and have humility. You can connect with God. You are never beyond Him. This is a truth Elder Holland so poetically expressed when he said, "It is not possible for you to sink lower than the infinite light of the Atonement shines."[85]

Sufficient humility moves us toward Heavenly Father and Jesus Christ. It moves us toward truth. It moves us toward salvation. In the moment, though we live in a crazy world, if we have humility, it can feel like home.

85   Jeffrey R. Holland, *Laborers in the Vineyard*, General Conference (Salt Lake City: The Church of Jesus Christ of Latter-day Saints), April 2012, Gospel Library App.

CHAPTER 6

Sufficient Repentance

THERE ARE A FEW THINGS I REMEMBER CLEARLY ABOUT MY BAPTISMAL day. It was a sunny September day in 1979. The powder blue bows in my hair that matched the dress my mother sewed for me, my white baptismal dress that floated up in the cold water, and the determination I felt to stay clean and pure for the rest of my life. I wasn't going to make any mistakes. I was going to be post-baptism perfect, and knowing I was going to stay that way lifted me to a spiritual high.

As we drove home, my grandpa suggested we stop to get donuts. With my eight-year-old, fresh-out-of-the-water righteous indignation, I raised my voice at my grandpa. How dare he suggest we buy donuts on the Sabbath? Didn't he know I was just baptized and didn't want to sin?

He softly replied, "Michelle. It's Saturday."

My heart sank as I realized I had just committed my first sin. I wasn't perfect anymore, and never would be. Tears fell as I accepted that I could repent, but I would never be completely clean and pure again.

Despite being taught well by my parents, I didn't understand repentance then. Not fully. I thought repentance was the hole left in a board by a removed nail. Repentance was apologizing for hitting your brother or lying to your mom and promising you'd never do it again. Or saying sorry to the grandpa you just yelled at for no good reason. Needless to say, I said sorry a lot in my early years.

As a teen, repentance grew into a formula of alliteration to obliterate sin, easy to remember steps to make sure my repentance was complete: recognition, remorse, restitution, and refusal to return to the sin. The formula was good, and backed by solid principles, but my view of repentance didn't reach much further beyond. My dad was my bishop during these years. I sat in his office a few times checking off the list of R's. I wanted to do better, to be better.

But, when I was seventeen years old, something happened that broke open my sheltered world and my narrow perspective of the gospel. A young man I had casually dated committed suicide. Our plan was to meet up at a Halloween party. I showed up. He never did.

His death ignited a storm of questions in my teenage mind. Why would God let him die? Where was my friend now? Was there still a chance for him? Did I believe there as hope for him? For me?

I poured my thoughts into my journal. There, I came to realize that I didn't know as much about the plan of happiness and the gospel as I thought I had. I didn't know God like I thought I had. I didn't know Jesus like I thought I had. I had been taught, but honestly, I had never taken the time to really learn. And it shook me.

For the first time in my life, I realized the truths I had been casually holding onto since I was a Sunbeam were the truths that would save my friend. The truths that would save me. I didn't feel as close to them as I thought I had been. I didn't feel as close to Heavenly Father and Jesus Christ as I thought I was.

In that moment, I realized I wanted to know more. I wanted to know *Them* more. I wanted to learn, to feel, to change. And so, I turned toward Them and moved in Their direction.

A realization. A change of desire. A choice. A movement toward the divine.

This is repentance.

I'll elaborate this idea with a confession. When I'm watching a TV show or movie, I have a pet peeve. Okay, two really.

My first pet peeve is when someone is performing CPR on some poor guy on the floor and a person (usually not a medical professional) tells them to stop because it's "too late." This premature and unqualified command is usually accompanied by a sad but firm, "They're gone," as they shake their head in dismay. I watch this and yell at the TV, "Do you not *watch* TV shows yourself?" How many times does the one performing CPR the call to stop and go on to revive the guy on the floor? In my own life, I have vowed to never be a "they're gone" girl.

It's the second pet peeve that bothers me the most. It's when one person is trying to run to or after another person, usually someone they love, to either help or embrace them, and then someone else grabs their arms and holds them back while they say something like, "Let them go," or "It's for the best."

To me, this pet peeve scenario is a simplified, albeit irritating, representation of sin. I want to be with Jesus and my sins are holding me back.

Now, in this TV/movie scenario, the person being held usually fights against the arms that hold them back. They cry. They yell. Then they do one of three things: they give up, they get angry and run away, or they break free from their oppressor and run toward the person they love.

Option three is like repentance.

Sin, complacency, distraction, or neglect can hold us back from Jesus. Repentance breaks us free.

I love this simplistic, visual approach. It works for me. Maybe it does for you too. It helps me understand it better.

So often, the mention of repentance can conjure a negative reaction. Maybe it's guilt or shame. Or maybe we feel a twinge of obligation, or hopelessness. Some have told me they feel repentance means they aren't good enough. Some have said it makes them feel like God's love is conditional. Some have said they don't need to repent at all, that God loves them exactly how they are and would never ask them to apologize or change.

But here is what I've learned. Repentance is not self-flogging. It is not proof we are broken and need to be fixed. Repentance *is the way* we come to Christ because that's where we *want* to be. That's where *He* wants us to be, with Him.

When I lost my friend, I wasn't steeped in grievous sin. But I had allowed the distractions of pride, insecurity, procrastination, complacency, and worldliness to hold me in place. His passing opened my eyes to what I was lacking, to what I wanted, to what I needed. The moment

I saw what I needed in my life clearly, the struggle to break free from what was holding me back and move toward God began—the real repentance began.

Repentance isn't a hole in a board or a formula to follow. It is our desire and effort to reunite with deity. Repentance is the struggle to break free from the grasp of sin and other things that hold us back so that we can move in the direction of Jesus Christ.

The Power of Re

My relationship with and understanding of repentance have continued to grow throughout my life. It has moved from an admission of guilt or a cause for shame to a blessed journey toward forgiveness.

Years ago, at the beginning of a Gospel Principles class, the class members and I were discussing repentance. I wrote *repentance* on the board followed by *redeem* and *reunite*. We talked about the beauty of each of these words. Then, noticing they shared the first two letters in each word, we decided to make a list of other gospel and repentance words that start with "re."

The list started out strong. Redemption. Redirect. Reignite. Reinvigorate. Remember.

And it kept growing. Relief. Reflect. Reverence. Renew. Reunite.

Seeing we were on a roll, we scrapped the scheduled lesson and kept going. Religion. Reform. Realization. Rely. Reflect. Remain. Recover. Respond. Reach. Rescue. Refuge.

By the end of the class, the entire board was filled with words that started with "re." It was powerful. On the top of the board I wrote, *The Power of Re*.

"Re" means *again*. That is such a powerful word, especially when we are talking about all the agains brought about by Jesus Christ and His Atonement. To be new again. To be united again. To feel peace again. To be close to Jesus again and again and again.

This is important because we will mess up again and again and again. It's a fact of our mortal state. We will be re-offenders until we die. But Jesus Christ will always be our Redeemer. His grace changes us, purifies us, and allows us to be forgiven again and again and again.

President Nelson spoke of this gift of change through repentance one Christmas season not too long ago. He explained that Greek was the original language of the New Testament. The word that was translated as "repent," when used in the context of the Savior calling people to repent, is *metanoeo*. When you split the word up, *meta* means *change* (like metamorphosis) and *noeo* means *mind*. President Nelson explained, that *noeo* is also associated with "knowledge," "breath," and "spirit."

He then pulled it all together in this hopeful testimony of what repentance is:

> Can we begin to see the breadth and depth of what the Lord is giving to us when He offers us the gift *to repent*? He invites us to change our minds, our knowledge, our spirit, even our breathing . . . Repentance is a resplendent gift. It is a process never to be feared. It is a gift for us to receive with joy and to use—even embrace—day after day as we seek to become more like our Savior.[86]

One of the Hebrew words most often used in the Old Testament for repentance is *shub*, meaning *to turn back to*. When we repent, we are returning our hope, our thoughts, our desires, and our hearts to Him.

How can we describe repentance?

Gift. Turn to. Change. Submission. Run to. Embrace. Peace.

Can you see the beauty in it?

Perhaps this is what the Savior was inviting us to do what He said, "Come unto me, all ye that are heavy laden, and I will give you rest."[87]

I love the "re" word President Nelson used to describe repentance: resplendent. It's so fitting.

Repentance is our liberation from the things that hold us back, even for just a moment. It is our desire to be with God, our choice to rush toward Jesus—to feel Them, to hear Them, to become like Them. It is a celebration, a reunion, a restoration of our souls.

It's revitalizing. It's rejuvenating. It's remarkable.

It is repentance.

---

86   Nelson R. M., *Four Gifts that Jesus Christ Offers to You*, First Presidency Christmas Devotional, Salt Lake City, 2018, https://www.churchofjesuschrist.org/media/video/2018-12-0040-president-russell-m-nelson?lang=eng.

87   Matthew 11:28.

Sufficient Repentance

I love focusing on the simplicity of the gospel and the hope and power it brings. It's one of the reasons I really loved teaching the Gospel Principles class. I also loved those who attended the class—long-time members, new converts, and good folks investigating the gospel. They were at different levels of understanding and spirituality from different backgrounds and situations. And yet, we came together each Sunday for the same reason: to learn about Heavenly Father and Jesus Christ.

I loved teaching about the beautiful gospel and the Church—faith, baptism, Holy Ghost, the priesthood, the plan of salvation, and more. It was a privilege to see minds and hearts open to truth, change, and love. But I especially loved teaching about repentance.

Many of the class members had some stumbling blocks and barricades. Some couldn't get past a piece of Church history they'd heard about. Others couldn't give up coffee. Others couldn't let go of the church they grew up in. And others simply didn't want to spend three hours in church each Sunday.

But the greatest stumbling block for those in my class—members and investigators alike—was their understanding of the concepts of sin, the Savior, and especially repentance. Many saw themselves as awful people, stained by the transgression of Adam and Eve. They viewed themselves as broken, dirty, and beyond saving. They would never be perfect, and therefore why should they try? Or they'd accepted their life was only to try everyday knowing they would only fail. In all cases, their pain brought my heart pain.

Throughout those years, I would often draw a set of stairs on the white board. I would draw a man near the top of the stairs looking down and a man at the bottom of the stairs looking up. I would then ask the class, if the top of the stairs was the ultimate goal, which man was in the better position?

Invariably they'd say the man near the top—a reasonable answer. He was almost there, after all. I would then paraphrase this quote by Hugh Nibley:

> Who is righteous? Anyone who is repenting. No matter how bad he
> has been, if he is repenting, he is a righteous man. There is hope for

him. And no matter how good he has been all his life, if he is not repenting, he is a wicked [or natural] man. The difference is which way you are facing. The man on the top of the stairs facing down is much worse off than the man on the bottom of the step who is facing up. The direction we are facing, that is repentance.[88]

A look. A step in the right direction. This is repentance.

The beauty of sufficient repentance is expressed passionately by an unexpected man. Not a prophet, but a killer turned convert: King Lamoni. After the conversion of himself, his wife, and much of his Lamanite kingdom, they collectively turn away from their warring ways and face God. The blood stains on their hands, their swords, and hearts are real, and so is the struggle from sin to Jesus.

What does it take to repent of the horrible things they had done? Listen to what King Lamoni says about all of them.

It has been all that we could do (as we were the most lost of all mankind) to repent of all our sins and the many murders which we have committed, and to get God to take them away from our hearts, for it was all we could do to repent *sufficiently* before God that he would take away our stain.[89]

What did their sufficient repentance look like? For King Lamoni, it takes being struck down for three days and three nights. For his wife, it takes seeing him that way. For many of their followers, it only takes hearing the word.

Each of their paths to and processes of repentance are different. But what they have in common is that each of them started where they were and did what they needed to do in that moment to push away from sin and run toward Jesus. They each have repentance sufficient for the Lord.

Think about that for a moment, then think about what it means for you. We are all in different places. Maybe you're in a place of obedient discipleship and have minor daily adjustments to make. Maybe you're in a place that's so dark you can't see a way out. Maybe you

---

88   Hugh Nibley, *Approaching Zion: The Collected Works of Hugh Nibley*, vol. 9, (Salt Lake City: Deseret Book Company & Provo: Foundation for Ancient Research and Mormon Studies), 1989.

89   Alma 24:11, italics added.

feel trapped by habitual sin and feel hopeless. Maybe you've discovered misplaced priorities or identities. Or maybe you're realizing there are things you've been neglecting to do that are holding you back from Him. It doesn't matter where you are because when you turn to face Jesus, He will be reaching for you. What matters is that *you* choose to face Him in this moment, that you want Him, that you engage in the struggle to break free and run to Him.

In Chapter 2, I mentioned a powerful truth taught by Amulek, the man who may very well have qualified himself as *bad* before he meets Alma. He speaks of one of the most hope-filled promises in the scriptures when he says,

> [F]or behold, now is the time and the day of your salvation: and therefore, if ye will repent and harden not your hearts, immediately shall the great plan of redemption be brought about unto you.[90]

Amulek loves repentance. In fact, the first thing he testifies of is the necessity of a redemption.[91]

There are a few things I love about this. First, he is talking to a group of people—his people—who have chosen a path which leads them away from God and into themselves. They are a wicked and arrogant lot, but they are *his* lot. Chances are, he knows some or even many of them personally. Chances are, he loves them. After he has experienced the sweetness of repentance himself, he offers them the greatest hope he can: that through the Atonement, they can change too. Through repentance, they can be closer to the Savior.

However, what I love the most is the time frame of the relief of redemption through repentance. Amulek doesn't say, "Well, you need to repent and change and prove yourself, *then* God will be there for you." No. He says, "*immediately* shall the great plan of redemption be brought about unto you."

One could paraphrase this as saying: "The *moment* you change your mind and will is the very moment the Lord can begin to change your heart."

Immediately. Now. In this moment.

---

90   Alma 34:31.
91   see Alma 34:8-10.

You don't have to wait until you're worthy to turn to Jesus. You don't need to be clean or pure. None of the people Jesus heals are whole to begin with. None of the people Jesus forgives are sinless. None of the people Jesus loves are perfect. All the people He invites to come to Him have issues, weaknesses, and faults, each one of them.

President Nelson taught the power of *now* when he said, "Yes, we should learn from the past, and yes, we should prepare for the future. But only *now* can we do. *Now* is the time we can learn. *Now* is the time we can repent."[92]

One thing I've learned is that Jesus isn't hoping for me or you to be worthy of Him someday. He hopes we choose to turn to Him, to follow Him, to be with Him today. Now.

What If?

A few years ago, I followed a prompting and reached out to a friend of mine to see how she was doing. It turned out, she was not doing well. Due to some poor decisions she had made, she was in a very challenging situation and couldn't see a way out. The flood of mixed emotions was nearly suffocating. She knew much of her suffering was her own fault. She wanted to have faith that God would help her solve the problem. But she was afraid (and even angry) that He might not help her, and she might have to suffer the painful consequences of her own choices.

She wanted so badly to connect with God, to feel Him, to hear Him, to be embraced by Him, but she couldn't. What if she wasn't worthy or deserving to pray and ask for help? So she didn't. And then, feelings of fear, confusion, shame, doubt, and abandonment followed.

I've felt this way before, when I knew it was my own thoughts and choices that were holding me back. In those times, I, too, didn't feel I deserved the privilege to pray or repent. It is a sad and scary place to be and begs questions like:

- What if I'm not worthy to access blessings or exercise faith because my suffering is my own fault?

---

92   Nelson R. M., *Now is the Time*, General Conference, Salt Lake City, April 2022, Gospel Library App.

- What if I backslide and make the same mistake again and again and again?
- What if repentance won't work for me.

All these questions can be combined into one great question: What if I don't feel I can come to God and be changed and forgiven?

The answer to this complicated question is simple. Come to Him anyway.

Elder Uchtdorf gave a longer, more eloquent answer. He said,

> My beloved brothers and sisters, dear friends, we all drift from time to time. But we can get back on course. We can navigate our way through the darkness and trials of this life and find our way back to our loving Heavenly Father if we seek and accept the spiritual landmarks He has provided, embrace personal revelation, and strive for daily restoration.[93]

Daily restoration born in moments. This is the power of sufficient.

Regardless of whether your need for repentance comes from the natural man in you, your weakness, or poor choices, the answer is the same. Come to Him every day. This is where we will find relief, change, strength, peace, forgiveness, and salvation.

Jesus teaches it this way: "But he that remaineth steadfast and is not overcome [by iniquity], the same shall be saved."[94] Jesus doesn't say we need to be perfect before we repent. He says "steadfast." To me, this means we strive to have sufficient moments over and over again, moments where we don't let our *what if* questions hold us back.

Maybe this means we change our *what if* questions.

What if God really would hear my prayers?

What if the Atonement will work for me?

What if I can change?

What if I can be forgiven?

What if there is hope for me after all?

These questions come from a place of hope, humility, and faith. The answers can bring the joy, peace, strength, and resilience needed

---

93   Dieter F. Uchtdorf, *Daily Restoration*, General Conference, (Salt Lake City: The Church of Jesus Christ of Latter-day Saints), October 2021, Gospel Library App.

94   JS Matthew 1:11.

in the repentance process because, as beautiful as repentance is, it isn't always easy.

I wish I could say the process was a quick ethereal journey through feel-good epiphanies and warm-fuzzy revelations. But I can't. Change takes time and some necessary things like the sting of regret, the guilt of recognition, the sorrow of pain caused, and the grief at what we lost. But, as Elder Maxwell so succinctly said, "There can be no real repentance without personal suffering and the passage of sufficient time for the needed cleansing and turning."[95]

Back to my friend from the beginning of the chapter. After talking with me and others, and much internal struggle, she did turn to the Lord. She felt Him near. And, as her problems began to sort out, with time and distance, she was able to look back and see that He had never left. She turned to Him more fully, with a new-found commitment, she worked hard, and He welcomed her with open arms.

There is work to be done. Becoming gods and goddesses is not an easy task. So when—not if—the requisite suffering comes, asking the right *what if* questions can be a soothing balm to our aching hearts and give us the strength and motivation to stay engaged.

Perhaps one of the most powerful what-if questions we can ask is, "What if I don't have to do this alone?" Brother Bradley R. Wilcox answers this with these comforting words: "Remember change is possible, repentance is a process, and worthiness is not flawlessness. Most important, remember that God and Christ are willing to help us right here and now."[96]

What if I don't have to do this alone? You don't!

What if God is really listening to you? He is!

What if you are as valued and loved as He says you are? You are!

What if you can repent when you make the same mistake again and again? You can!

What if God can help and forgive you, even if your pain is your own fault? He can!

95   Neal A. Maxwell, *Repentance*, General Conference (Salt Lake City: The Church of Jesus Christ of Latter-day Saints, October 1991), Gospel Library App.

96   Bradley R. Wilcox, *Worthiness Is Not Flawlessness*, General Conference (Salt Lake City: The Church of Jesus Christ of Latter-day Saints), October 2021, Gospel Library App.

What if the Atonement of Jesus Christ really does work? It does!

Repentance can be hard, but it is always glorious! So glorious that the Shepherd and Heaven rejoice over just one person that repents.[97] That one person is you.

Doesn't this make you feel joy? I feel it. I love that "men are that they might have joy."[98] I think repentance is, in large part, how we feel that joy. As Elder Bednar explains, "Because of Heavenly Father's plan and the Savior's Atonement, sincere repentance invites us to turn to and depend upon Jesus Christ, the true source of joy."[99]

Elder Dale G. Renlund wants us to feel joy as well. He said,

> I invite you to feel more joy in your life: joy in the knowledge that the Atonement of Jesus Christ is real; joy in the Savior's ability, willingness, and desire to forgive; and joy in choosing to repent. Let us follow the instruction to 'with joy . . . draw water out of the wells of salvation,' [Isaiah 12:23]. May we choose to repent, forsake our sins, and turn our hearts and wills around to follow our Savior.[100]

Break free from what's holding us back, turn toward our Savior, and run to be with Him now and over and over again. This is sufficient and sweet repentance.

Give Him Your Sufficient

The gospel of Jesus Christ is a gospel of transformation. I heard someone once say that if you aren't changing, you're not living the gospel. This rings true to me. Elder Dallin H. Oaks shared a similar sentiment when we said, "The gospel of Jesus Christ challenges us to *become* something"[101]

---

97   see Luke 15:6-7.

98   2 Nephi 2:25.

99   Bednar, David A., *That They Might Have Joy*, BYU Speeches, Provo, December 4, 2018, https://speeches.byu.edu/talks/david-a-bednar/that-they-might-have-joy/.

100   Dale G. Renlund, *Repentance: A Joyful Choice*, General Conference (Salt Lake City: The Church of Jesus Christ of Latter-day Saints), October 2016, Gospel Library App.

101   Dallin H. Oaks, *The Challenge to Become*, General Conference (Salt Lake City: The Church of Jesus Christ of Latter-day Saints), October 2000, Gospel Library App.

Elder Bednar expressed it this way:

> The grand objective of the Savior's gospel was summarized suc-
> cinctly by President David O. McKay (1873–1970): 'The purpose of
> the gospel is . . . to make bad men good and good men better, and to
> change human nature.' Thus, the journey of mortality is to progress
> from bad to good to better and to experience the mighty change of
> heart—to have our fallen natures changed."[102]

Because of Jesus Christ, we get to repent. We get to change. We get
to grow. We get to transform. We have the opportunity to reach our
potential, to become like Him and our heavenly parents. We don't have
to be enough ourselves. We get to be perfect in Jesus Christ. Having
sufficient hope, faith, and humility to culminate in repentance is the
key to unlocking that power.

I will say this again. We don't have to do or be enough for Jesus.
We simply need to have enough to desire to be near Him. Then He will
do the changing.

Give Him your fear and He will give you strength.

Give Him your doubts and He will give you peace.

Give Him your pride and He will give you wisdom.

Give Him your sins and He will give you forgiveness.

Give Him your heart and He will give you a new one.

Give Him your sufficient and He will give you His all.

---

102   David A. Bednar, *The Atonement and the Journey of Mortality*, General Conference
(Salt Lake City: The Church of Jesus Christ of Latter-day Saints) April 2012, Gospel
Library App.

PART TWO: Their Sufficient

CHAPTER 7

Sufficient Grace

ON THE AFTERNOON OF JULY 6TH, 2010, I WAS CLEANING OUT MY DOWN-stairs closet. My cleaning/reorganizing process, much to the chagrin of my tidy husband, is simple: I pull everything out of the closet, throw some away, donate some, and put the rest back in the closet. He loves the end result, but it's the middle that's hard, when every single thing that was behind the closed door is now strung across our family room.

This particular Tuesday was no exception. The couches and floor were littered with place mats, platters, aprons, a vacuum, a broom, a carpet rake (only *the* best investment ever), lint brushes, a blood-pressure cuff, dog treats, flashlights, and literally dozens more random things that had been shoved into the closet under the stairs during that past year. My family room looked like a grave site for garage sale rejects.

I was neck deep in the rubble when my phone rang. The woman introduced herself as Kristen, a social worker.

It's funny how God works.

The night before my hysterectomy, ten years and one month before this closet-cleaning occasion, I received a blessing in which I was told I wasn't finished adding to my family. I reassured God I was and reminded Him I wasn't going in for a tonsillectomy, but a complete hysterectomy. About eight years later, adoption entered my heart. My husband and I became licensed foster/adopt parents, researched a lot of kids, met some kids, and even fostered two boys. We loved those boys.

But a month after they moved in with us, God told me they weren't mine—a story I dive deeper into in my book *Leaning on Jesus: Strength for a Woman's Heart*. We found the home God wanted for them, but I was heartbroken. My heart couldn't take it, so we decided to let our license expire. I told God I was done.

And then Kristen called. She found our family information sheet on her desk and wanted to know if we would take an emergency placement child for three nights. She explained it was a strange request for two reasons. One, she had never seen our family sheet before, nor had anyone in her office. It just seemed to have appeared on her desk. Two, even though she wasn't familiar with our family, she felt she needed to call us.

I asked for a few minutes to check with my family. I called Jerey, Spencer, and Paige. We talked and prayed about it. Then I called Kristen and told her we would take the child, but only for three days. I hung up the phone, shoved every single random thing back in my closet, and got ready for her arrival.

Six hours later Kristen walked through my door with the cutest little six-year-old blonde girl named Victoria in tow. Victoria had a juice mustache and a bag of Wendy's. She flashed me a nervous smile, then sat by Paige on the floor and watched *The Little Mermaid* while Kristen and I talked.

"Three days," I reminded her. My heart wasn't strong enough for anything more.

"Three days," she replied.

Three days later Kristen called. "We are having a hard time finding a foster placement. Can you do just two weeks more?"

After talking with the family and praying, I replied, "Two weeks. But only two weeks."

I was already starting to love this girl, but there were family complications, she had struggles, and I didn't feel I had the strength to give much more. My heart was still tender and tired.

One night, somewhere in those two weeks, I was tucking her in bed when God whispered to me that she was mine.

My first response was no.

You can judge me. That's okay. But to a tired and scared heart, even good things can feel like too much.

God again assured me she was mine.

After much prayer, Jerey and I felt it too.

On a pajama walk around the neighborhood one evening, I asked Victoria what she wanted. Even though she was six, I wanted her to feel like she had a voice. She chose us. We chose her. And so, we started the process of adoption.

As the adoption day approached, Victoria told me she wanted to change her name. She wanted a new name for her new life. So, I looked up the top 100 names for the year she was born. She narrowed them down to the top ten. I was campaigning hard for Emma Jane. Isn't that *the* cutest name? But she chose a different name. One that spoke to her.

She chose Grace.

Over the years, her name became so much more than just her name to me. With her permission, I can tell you raising her was challenging. Not only did she come wrapped in trauma, but her needs seemed to be directly related to everything I lacked. She became the physical embodiment of Ether 12:28: "Behold, I will show unto [Michelle] [her] weakness."

Over the years, as I struggled with the challenges and demands of raising her, I was often reminded that God gave her to me not just so I could help her, but so that I could grow through her.

That was never more apparent than it was in church during the hymns. There were many Sunday where I was minding my own business, singing praises, when God would use my daughter's name to teach me. As I sang about God sending His "grace this holy day,"[103] I was reminded that my daughter was brought to me by God.

It was easy to sing of how I was "confused at the grace that so fully He proffers me"[104] on those Sundays I struggled to understand why God would ask me, with all my imperfections, to raise this girl when there were so many other women who could do it so much better.

103 "God Our Father, Hear Us Pray," *Hymns of the Church of Jesus Christ of Latter-day Saints*, Salt Lake City: The Church of Jesus Christ of Latter-day Saints, 1985.
104 "I Stand All Amazed," *Hymns of the Church of Jesus Christ of Latter-day Saints*, Salt Lake City: The Church of Jesus Christ of Latter-day Saints, 1985.

On good days, I'd happily sing about how "the flow'rs of grace appear."[105]

And then there was the Sunday when I knew I wasn't good enough. As I sang of God's "works of grace, how bright they shine,"[106] I was gently and unmistakably reminded that God's grace would save me, and my daughter, Grace, was a vehicle for His grace.

I didn't understand ten years ago when my daughter chose her name how important her name would become in my life. How it would serve as a constant reminder that I can be who she needs me to be *because* of God's grace. And when I am not who she needs me to be, His grace can strengthen her and help her grow.

Through my daughter, I've come to understand grace in ways I never did before. I can now see the rest of Ether 12:28 in myself: "Behold, I will show unto [Michelle] [her] weakness, and I will show unto [her] that faith, hope, and charity bringing unto me—the fountain of all righteousness."

My daughter's needs brought me to my knees over and over again. There, I offered my sufficient hope, faith, humility, and so much repentance. And there, through my daughter, God gave me grace. *She* led me to God's grace.

Through His grace, He gave me what I lacked. He gave me what I needed. Through His grace, He gave me love, strength, perspective, and forgiveness. Through His grace He allowed me to change and grow, to transform again and again and again.

I love the way Bother Wilcox explained grace to a student who was struggling to understand it. In a talk he gave almost one year to the day after my daughter walked through my door, Brother Wilcox shared that "Jesus doesn't make *up* the difference. Jesus makes *all* the difference. Grace is not about filling gaps. It is about filling us."[107]

---

105   "There Is Sunshine in My Soul Today," *Hymns of the Church of Jesus Christ of Latter-day Saints*, Salt Lake City: The Church of Jesus Christ of Latter-day Saints, 1985.

106   "Sweet Is the Work," *Hymns of the Church of Jesus Christ of Latter-day Saints*, Salt Lake City: The Church of Jesus Christ of Latter-day Saints, 1985.

107   Bradley R. Wilcox, *His Grace Is Sufficient,* BYU Speeches delivered July 12, 2011, accessed May 1 2023, https://speeches.byu.edu/talks/brad-wilcox/his-grace-is-sufficient/.

I felt that through my daughter, Grace. And I have felt that through God's grace.

Sufficient Grace

A few months after my mom had passed away, I was still in the grips of grief. It was at the end of a long day of failures where I was tired and had been less patient than normal. The house was a mess, my creative well had long-dried up, I hadn't exercised in a week, and I snapped at my family. I couldn't take another minute of being a failure as a wife, a mom, a person. I got in my car and drove, ending up in an empty far corner of a large parking lot.

The chasm between who I saw myself as and who I thought I should be filled with a flash flood of negative and painful waves. I wasn't strong enough. I wasn't good enough. I've ruined my children. I'm not helping anyone. I've failed them. I have nothing to offer. As I cried, I cataloged all my weaknesses and faults, confirming the idea that I am, indeed, an imperfect and undeserving mess. Finally, exhausted, I leaned my head against the window and prayed. I apologized to God for my failings. I was sure I had disappointed Him more than anyone else. The prayer was as eloquent and heartfelt as my tired soul allowed.

Then, something happened.

I felt . . . still . . . and warm.

In that moment, God spoke to me in a language I could understand. It wasn't in words or sentences. It wasn't even an overwhelming feeling of relief. It was small feeling, one that was familiar, comfortable, and safe. And it came with a tender mercy of understanding. He wasn't disappointed in me. I wasn't failing. I would be okay. Everything else would be okay.

Then I felt something I wasn't expecting. I felt He wanted me to be gentle with myself. I was still young and still learning. Yes, I was struggling with elements of life, but that struggle was a part of life. I wasn't alone in the struggle. I was His child. He would help me. He already was.

I don't understand how the Atonement works. I just know it does. Through Jesus's atoning sacrifice, our debt is paid, and we will be resurrected. When I was younger, I thought this was what the Atonement was for—to free us from sin and be forgiven. But there is more, so much more.

That more is grace.

That is what I felt in the car that night. It was the feeling He gave, the thought He offered, the tenderness He showed, and the pain He lessened. It was the help I needed from heaven.

Elder Uchtdorf defines grace as "the divine assistance and endowment of strength by which we grow from the flawed and limited beings we are now into exalted beings."[108]

We are meant to become exalted beings. This life isn't about being perfect, but becoming a perfect being, our full-grown spiritual selves. This transformation only happens at the corner of agency and grace—where our sufficient hope, faith, humility, and repentance meet His sufficient grace. This is where we become whole.

Sometimes I can't wrap my brain around it. *I* have the potential to be a goddess. It feels so . . . strange. I'm painfully aware of my weaknesses, faults, mistakes, and bad choices. I clearly see the enormous chasm that stretches between where I am and where God says I can be. I see the pride that keeps me from connecting with God and with others. I see the doubts that trespass on my faith and the insecurity I feel despite the earthly and heavenly validation I receive. My mind often vacillates between two extremes—*Do you know who I am?* and *It doesn't matter who I am.* I am everything, and I am nothing. I get frustrated at this dichotomy, more proof of my wild imperfection and under-serving nature. Doesn't sound like goddess material to me.

And yet, somehow to God it is. We are all gods and goddesses in the making to Him.

Our imperfections don't scare Him. Our weaknesses don't cause Him to pause. Our sins don't surprise Him.

We are His children living His plan exactly the way He knew we would.

He sees us as toddler gods and goddess, falling forward in His plan toward perfection in Christ. A plan that includes divine help. So much

108   Dieter F. Uchtdorf, *The Gift of Grace*, General Conference (Salt Lake City: The Church of Jesus Christ of Latter-day Saints), April 2015, Gospel Library App.

help. Not just to reach exaltation, but on every step of the journey there. We just need to receive it.

I love the last three verses of the Book of Mormon. At this point, Moroni has been through a lot. He has lost his family and friends in a long, bloody war, then is left to wander for thirty-six more years, alone, witnessing the carnage and wickedness of the Lamanites as he finishes compiling the records his father started, and even adding some of his own. He is a man well acquainted with grief and struggle.

Out of everything Moroni could have ended his record with— spiritual experiences, more doctrine, paternal advice, etc.—he chooses to talk about perfection, real perfection. The kind that only comes through agency and grace. He implores us with these moving words:

> Yea, come unto Christ and be perfected in him . . . and deny your-
> selves of all ungodliness (*so, turn away from the things that are holding
> you back from the Savior*) and if (*there's the agency*) ye shall deny your-
> selves of all ungodliness, and love God with all of your might, mind
> and strength, *then* is his grace sufficient for you, that by his grace ye
> may be perfect in Christ.[109]

There are a couple of things we should notice in this verse. Do you see the if/then formula? If we choose Him, then His grace is sufficient. It's important to understand that grace isn't being held hostage until we check off the list in this verse. Grace doesn't take effect only after we've done all we can do. What Moroni is saying is that the fulness of God's grace *won't* take effect *until* we let it. Giving our heart to God is giving Him permission to change it. He won't change a locked heart. He won't change an unwilling person.

One of my favorite books on grace is called *Original Grace*, written by Adam S. Miller. His take on grace had a profound effect on me. In essence, his message is that grace is not a backup plan, but *the* plan. Because it is the plan, it is readily available to anyone who wants it. Miller said,

> There is no secret to grace. It can be resisted or embraced. If I resist
> grace, I cut myself off from it. This is sin. If I embrace grace, I'll find

---

109   Moroni 10:32.

myself giving it. This is the straight path, the direct route that leads immediately to salvation.[110]

The other thing we should notice in Moroni's verse is the little two-letter word: "in." It gives perfection its true position and process. We become perfect *in* Jesus Christ. With Him. Through Him. Because of Him and His grace. The burden of perfection does not belong to us. The opportunity of perfecting us belongs to Jesus Christ alone. Elder Holland reminds us that

> our only hope for true perfection is receiving it as a gift from heaven—we can't 'earn' it. Thus, the grace of Christ offers us not only salvation from sorrow and sin and death but also salvation from our own persistent self-criticism.[111]

We don't have to beat ourselves up. We can put the bats down and pick up grace instead. The Lord's grace is sufficient to perfect, complete, or make whole. His grace is also sufficient to give us divine aid as we move along that path toward and with Him.

His grace is sufficient to heal, to comfort, to teach, to motivate, to stretch, to calm, to whisper, to strengthen . . . to give us what we need in our moments of need as well as our moments of want. Accepting grace isn't about making up the deficit left by our mortal state because we are broken or not enough. It's not a backup plan. As Adam S. Miller says, "a grace-filled partnership with Christ *is* the original plan, full-stop—not an unfortunate intervention necessitated by my failure to save myself."[112]

When we live in a grace-filled partnership with Christ, we can receive divine help in challenging moments. Grace can look like added courage to repent, comfort in time of loss, hugging a child who's choosing a different path, or holding your head up high when shame wants to hold it down.

---

110   Adam S. Miller, Original Grace, (Provo: BYU Maxwell Institute & Salt lake City: Deseret Book Company) 2022.

111   Jeffrey R. Holland, *Be Ye Therefore Perfect—Eventually*, General Conference (Salt Lake City: The Church of Jesus Christ of Latter-day Saints), October 2017, Gospel Library App.

112   Adam S. Miller, Original Grace, (Provo: BYU Maxwell Institute & Salt lake City: Deseret Book Company) 2022.

It looks like courage, strength, answers, and impressions. It looks like tolerance, discipline, patience, or forgiveness.

It looks like love, joy, connection, and change.

God's grace is sufficient for everything we need.

It seems unfair that we give God our imperfect hearts and He gives us His perfect Son and His perfect grace, but that is the perfect plan.

In the quest for perfection in Christ, alone we can't reach it. But, with grace we can. Paul taught this truth two thousand years ago when he said, "Not that we are sufficient of ourselves to think any thing as of ourselves; but our sufficiency is of God."[113]

Grace is what helps us become sufficient of God. Especially when we realize that because of grace, we can seek for sufficient hope, faith, humility, and repentance in the first place. His grace is truly sufficient for us all.

Covenant Grace

Recently, during an institute class, we were talking about repentance and the question of grace and divine help came up. I asked a married couple to come to the front of the room and stand to my right. Then I picked a random young man and young woman to come and stand next to each other to my left. In a moment of levity, we took inventory of how these two pairs came together. The married couple were standing shoulder to shoulder, holding hands. The other pair stood about six inches apart making a valiant effort to avoid any eye contact.

I asked the young man on my left what he would do if he needed five dollars and she had five dollars. He could ask to borrow some of her money, right? He shyly nodded.

I asked the same thing of the wife on my right. Her answer was different. There wasn't his or her money, just *their* money. She didn't have to ask because it was shared. "Besides," the wife added with a grin, "I'm the bread winner anyway." Her husband nodded, smiling; "It's true."

We talked as a class about the differences between these two pairs and it came down to a *covenant relationship*. One pair were two people

---

113   2 Corinthians 3:5.

with different lives sharing the same space; the other pair were two people sharing the same life.

I explained to the class that there are many people who are close to Jesus, who know Him and love Him. They can ask Him for help and He will help them as much as He can. He is their friend and loves them.

However, having a covenant relationship with Jesus Christ is different. We move from being near Him to sharing a life *with* Him. We experience a level of commitment and privilege that is only available in a covenant relationship, a divine partnership. Our understanding of ourselves and Him grow, as does our access to Him and, yes, His grace. Adam Miller emphasized that in his book.

> There aren't two kinds of perfection. The only kind of perfection is perfection-in-Christ. Perfection results from growing *deeper* into the grace of a divine partnership so that, as Christ put it, we 'all may be one; as thou, Father, art in me, and I in thee, that they may be one in us.' (John 17:21)[114]

This isn't new doctrine. Jacob rejoiced in this same principle nearly three thousand years ago: "My soul delighteth in the covenants of the Lord . . . yea, my soul delighteth in his grace, and his justice, and power, and mercy in the great and eternal plan of deliverance from death."[115]

The Lord Himself said, "if you keep my commandments you shall receive of [God's] fulness and be glorified in me as I am in the Father; therefore, I say unto you, you shall receive grace for grace."[116]

Heavenly Father and Jesus Christ don't just want us to have faith in Them. They don't want us to stand by Them and ask Them for help. They want us to be one with Them.

This is what Jesus prayed for in the literal last hours before His sacrifice and death. He prayed for His apostles and then us.

> Neither I pray for these alone, but for them also which shall believe on me through their word; that they all may be one, as thou, Father,

---

114   Adam S. Miller, Original Grace, (Provo: BYU Maxwell Institute & Salt lake City: Deseret Book Company) 2022.
115   2 Nephi 11:5.
116   D&C 93:20.

art in me, and I in thee, that they may be one *in* us . . . And the glory which thou gavest me I have given them; that they may be one, even as we are one: I in them, and thou in me, that they may be made perfect *in* one; and that the world may know that thou hast sent me, and hast loved them, as thou hast loved me.[117]

The Savior of the world wants to share His life with us, not casually, but by covenant.

We are made perfect—whole or complete—through the grace of a divine, covenant partnership. It makes sense. He can change us only as much as we want Him to. He can change our whole hearts only when we give Him our whole hearts. He can make us like Him if we choose a life like Him, and a life *with* Him.

I love that fact that the Lord wants a relationship with us. Elder D. Todd Christofferson said, "What our Heavenly Father offers us is Himself and His Son, a close and enduring relationship with Them through the grace and mediation of Jesus Christ, our Redeemer."[118]

President Nelson assures us that "entering into a covenant relationship with God binds us to Him in a way that makes *everything* about life easier." He continues:

> Please do not misunderstand me: I did *not* say that making covenants makes life *easy*. In fact, expect opposition, because the adversary does not want you to discover the power of Jesus Christ. But yoking yourself with the Savior means you have access to *His* strength and redeeming power.[119]

I love that the Lord wants us to be in a committed relationship with Him, where there are obligations, expectations, and blessings to be had. It's beautiful, yet, inequitable. He asks for our hearts, and He gives us everything we need to fill them with joy, wisdom, loved ones, and change. Through grace, He gives us all that we need as we give Him what He wants. "Behold," He said, "my grace is sufficient for you;

117 John 17:21-23, italics added.
118 D. Todd Christofferson, *Our Relationship with God*, General Conference (Salt Lake City: The Church of Jesus Christ of Latter-day Saints), April 2022, Gospel Library App.
119 Russell M. Nelson, *Overcome the World and Find Rest*, General Conference (Salt Lake City: The Church of Jesus Christ of Latter-day Saints), October 2022, Gospel Library App.

you must walk uprightly before me."[120] In another statement on grace, Adam Miller said,

> God's offer of grace takes the form of a covenant relationship with Christ. Grace, as a practical matter, is concretely expressed in this present-tense partnership. This partnership is, in turn, the means by which salvation is accomplished.[121]

When I married Jerey, I took his name to show we are one. Not was, but *are*. I entered a covenant relationship with him in 1995, but our covenant partnership is present tense. It is the same with the Lord. When we are baptized, we begin this journey by taking Jesus's name. Then, if we keep our end of the deal, that partnership stays in effect, every day.

Each Sunday as we partake of the sacrament, we renew our commitment to our shared life. We don't have to wonder or doubt how much He wants to be one with us; the proof is in the bread and the water. Each week we are reminded of the life we share with Him. In the temple, we can make even greater and deeper covenants, covenants that further bind us to Him and unlock the power of grace. We can deepen and broaden our present-tense, divine partnership with Him.

When I was called as a stake Relief Society president, I asked my stake president what he wanted the sisters to know. He told me that faith is wonderful, but the power we receive in this life comes through the covenants we make. That covenant power lets us share a life with Him as we become like Him.

That power is grace.

The Throne of Grace

I met Monique in 2013 while attending my first writers conference. We were roommates. She was tough, street smart, and said it like it was. As I got to know her over the years, I learned she had lived a life harder than I could imagine. She had grown up outside the gospel in an extremely toxic home. Her teenage years were filled with sex,

---

120   D&C 18:31.
121   Adam S. Miller, Original Grace, (Provo: BYU Maxwell Institute & Salt lake City: Deseret Book Company) 2022.

drugs, and alcohol to drown out the psychological and physical abuse she endured.

Monique also experienced the deep and sweet change that only grace can bring. Later in life she discovered the gospel and herself. Through moments of sufficient hope, faith, humility, and repentance, she came to know her Savior in a very real way. She sought Him in prayer, studied His character, and trusted the calming peace she felt that all would be well. She sought grace and let it change her.

Monique's relationship with her Savior didn't spare her from the challenges of life and the sacrifices that she felt she needed to make. She experienced a difficult divorce and cared for her parents, and a stepmother she loved, in their later years until they passed away. All through this, I watched as Monique continued to choose the things that kept her close to the Savior. She sought for His grace and embraced every ounce He had to give her as He strengthened her, guided her, supported her, and loved her.

Recently she said to me, "I am a living example of God's grace in action. And I love Him for it."[122] I can testify of this change.

Monique is a woman of wisdom and compassion, forgiveness and mercy. She is not perfect, but she knows what perfection is—a life with Heavenly Father and Jesus Christ as her companions. She did not wait passively for God to save her while she licked her wounds. She knew He had promised help, and she sought for it, expected it, and loved Him even more for it.

She is the living embodiment of one of my favorite verses in all scripture. "Let us therefore come boldly unto the throne of grace, that we may obtain mercy, and find grace to help in time of need."[123]

Despite understanding that grace is part of the plan and a gift to us from the beginning, we sometimes inch toward it apologetically as if we are inconveniencing the Lord. Maybe we feel we shouldn't need help or that we should be able to do life on our own. Or we may feel we don't deserve divine help. Or, perhaps, we look at grace through a scarcity lens, as if us asking for grace means we are taking His attention and grace away from others.

---

122   Facebook Comment by Hickman July 25, 2023.
123   Hebrews 4:16.

None of these are true.

The Lord wants us to come boldly to Him now and always to seek the grace He wants to give. The grace that's ours to claim in a shared life with Him.

I think of the story of Jesus in Luke 7:37-50 as He was dining in the house of a man named Simon. During the meal, an unnamed woman—a sinner—hears Jesus is there and comes into the home to find Him. She is uninvited but determined. She comes boldly to the throne of grace.

When she reaches Him, she weeps and washes His feet with her tears then dries them with her hair. Then she kisses and anoints His feet. How beautifully bold.

She doesn't ask permission. She makes no recorded apology. She simply knows where He is, longs to be with Him, and comes boldly to Him and then loves Him boldly.

And how does the Savior respond?

He gives her grace.

He forgives her sins then says, "Thy faith hath saved thee; go in peace."[124]

The only description we have of this woman is that she is a sinner. And still, she is rewarded for coming boldly to the throne of grace.

We are all sinners; we are all invited to come boldly to the throne of grace.

Elder Holland reminds us that

> there is no problem which you cannot overcome. There is no dream that in the unfolding of time and eternity cannot yet be realized. Even if you feel you are the lost and last laborer on the eleventh hour, the Lord of the vineyard still stands beckoning, 'Come boldly [to] the throne of grace,' and fall at the feet of the Holy One of Israel. Come and feast 'without money and without price' at the table of the Lord.[125]

Why does He beckon us to come boldly? Because we need to know that we need His grace and we can trust that we will receive it.

---

124   Luke 7:50.
125   Jeffrey R. Holland, *Laborers in the Vineyard*, General Conference (Salt Lake City: The Church of Jesus Christ of Latter-day Saints), April 2021, Gospel Library App.

I have come boldly before the throne of grace many times in my life and received grace. Two times come to mind. The first was a time-sensitive need, the second a life-sensitive need.

Recently I had a major life-decision to make. I had three equally appealing and viable opportunities in front of me, no idea which one to choose, and one day to decide. Each would take me and my family down a different path. And so, after doing my research, talking with my husband for hours, and praying, I still needed more information to make a sound decision. I needed divine help and I needed it now. I went to the temple alone. I prayed aloud on my way there, sharing every scenario, thought, and concern with God. Then I told God this afternoon temple trip was me boldly coming to the throne of grace in a time of need. I was seeking His promised help and was fully expecting to receive it. And I did.

Then, there was the time that was life-sensitive. With my daughter's permission, I share this next experience. One evening a few years ago, I was watching a show with my husband downstairs when Paige, then twenty years old, called to me from the second floor, asking me to come up and see her. I went upstairs, followed her into my room, and sat on my bed. "What's up?" I asked, thinking she wanted to talk about boys or school or something her sister had done that annoyed her. Standing in front of me, she extended her left arm toward me. Her wrist was slightly red and scratched. Laying on her open palm was a razor. "You need to take this," she said.

Time slowed. I looked at the razor then to my daughter's face as I prayed. It wasn't a plea for help. It was a bold demand. "God, give me the words to say and the help I need."

Peace and strength expanded inside of me like an inflating balloon. I was calm and unafraid. I smiled at my daughter, took the razor, and asked her to sit beside me. I don't remember what I said, but I remember God telling me what to say. I also remember the lack of fear I felt for her. God let me feel, let me know, she was going to be okay. And He was right. There have been some tough times, but Paige has never dipped that low again. It has been amazing to watch grace help her in so many of her times of need, giving her direction and perspective, strength, and peace. As of this writing, she is a week away from going boldly to the temple to enter into her own covenant relationship with the Lord. There will still be challenges ahead, but we both find peace knowing that grace will abound even more in her life.

This is grace. I had the right to ask for it boldly and in both situations, I received it sweetly and unmistakably.

Grace, however, doesn't always come in the form we want. Sometimes grace is a lost opportunity. Sometimes grace is love and sorrow at the loss of a loved one. Sometimes grace is a silent heaven. But grace is always what we need. Always.

During a lesson focused on what we have testimonies *of,* a good sister in my ward said, "*Of* is very directional. I love the idea that our testimonies aren't static. When we have a testimony *of* something, there is movement between us and the Savior. I have given to a principle and as a result received from the Lord. The more I can give to Christ, the more I can receive from Him." As we come boldly to the throne of grace, we can be sure we will be met with open arms. And we can choose to trust that, even if we can't see it, it will be given.

In fact, I think most times we aren't even aware of the grace that is woven through every moment of our lives. The Savior said to us, "Behold, ye are little children and ye cannot bear all things now; ye must grow in grace and in the knowledge of the truth" (D&C 50:40). We grow in grace, breath by breath. Grace is there even when we are holding our breath.

Every time we strive for sufficient hope and faith in Him, humility, and repentance, we are coming boldly before the throne of grace. And every time, the grace He gives us is sufficient to help, to lift, to teach, to transform. It is a beautiful reciprocal relationship.

God loves us. He has big plans for us, ones that we can't fully comprehend. Plans that rely on grace. This might create feelings of inadequacy or of falling short. Elder Maxwell said these are normal.

> There is no way the Church can honestly describe where we must yet go and what we must yet do without creating a sense of immense distance . . . This is a gospel of grand expectations, but God's grace is sufficient for each of us.[126]

---

126 Neal A. Maxwell, *Not Withstanding My Weakness,* General Conference (Salt Lake City: The Church of Jesus Christ of Latter-day Saints), October 1976, Gospel Library App.

We don't need to apologize for wanting or needing grace. We don't need to feel insecure or doubt. We don't have to worry about deserving it. God loves us. The Savior lived, died, and lives again for us. We are loved, wanted, and needed. *We* are Their work and their glory.[127]

Our transformation is an eternal one that won't come easy, but it's one that They are invested in right now. Brother Wilcox said it beautifully.

> The grace of Christ is sufficient—sufficient to cover our debt, sufficient to transform us, and sufficient to help us as long as that transformation process takes. The Book of Mormon teaches us to rely solely on "the merits, and mercy, and grace of the Holy Messiah" (2 Nephi 2:8). As we do, we do not discover—as some Christians believe—that Christ requires nothing of us. Rather, we discover the reason He requires so much and the strength to do all He asks (see Philippians 4:13). Grace is not the absence of God's high expectations. Grace is the presence of God's power (see Luke 1:37). . . I testify that God's grace is sufficient. Jesus' grace is sufficient . . . Seek Christ, and, as you do, I promise you will feel the enabling power we call His amazing grace.[128]

Through grace Their love is made manifest. It is sufficient for us, even if we feel we don't deserve it.

Whatever shortfall we may have, whatever weakness we may be keenly aware of, whatever mistakes we may make, grace is sufficient to transform them. Whatever disappointment we need to experience, whatever sorrow we must feel, whatever grief we must endure, grace is sufficient to soften and make use of them.

God's grace is sufficient for us to endure, enjoy, and become. His sufficient grace allows us to have sufficient hope, faith, humility, and repentance. It is there always, as Paul was so careful to include, and even more so in our covenant relationship with Him. And we have the privilege to receive it, embrace it, and yes, ask for it boldly.

---

127   see Moses 1:39.

128   Bradley R. Wilcox, *His Grace is Sufficient,* BYU Speeches delivered July 12, 2011, accessed May 1 2023, https://speeches.byu.edu/talks/brad-wilcox/his-grace-is-sufficient/.

When You Can't See Grace

What happens when we come boldly to the throne of grace and we don't feel we get what we are asking for?

What about the times we feel alone or weak? When we ask for help and it doesn't come?

What about other factors that might affect how we feel or see grace, like mental illness or deep emotions like anger or grief?

What happens when we find ourselves living a life so different than the one we had planned?

What if we are battling grief or loss that have carved a dark hole so large we feel we are falling into it?

What do we do if we can't feel or see grace?

We choose to believe it is still there.

I know. Not really a warm-fuzzy answer. But it's the truth. Regardless of the darkness or difficulties we face, grace is there.

Sometimes, I believe, sufficient hope and faith is to continue to move toward Him despite the lack of evidence of grace. We choose to trust God is there, that grace is there.

Choosing to trust in God and His ways can be scary. It involves vulnerability and a purposeful sacrifice of control. That is frightening because our walls and our effort to control can make us feel safe. They can mitigate variables and abate anxiety. From the false protection of this place, we peek over our walls for concrete reasons to come out. We check for empirical evidence that God should be trusted, that we can see His love, and that He really is there. And when we don't see it, we retreat once again.

Aside from fear, pain can keep us behind these walls. So can insecurity, doubt, shame, and a slew of other feel-bad feelings.

Trusting without evidence is hard. But trust we must.

When there are only one set of footprints in the sand, we can choose to believe He is carrying us.

Paul famously taught that "faith is the substance of things hoped for, the evidence of things not seen."[129] In other words, if you cannot

---

129   Hebrews 11:1.

see evidence for faith, let your faith be the evidence of the things you sometimes cannot see, like grace.

Elder Neil A. Anderson offered this suggestion: "Pray with all your heart. Strengthen your faith in Jesus Christ, in His reality, in His grace. Hold on to His words: 'My grace is sufficient for thee: for my strength is made perfect in weakness' (2 Corinthians12:9)."[130]

During those dark times when you might wonder if you have sunk below the reach of grace, know that grace's arms are long and strong.

If the darkness is caused by your own choices or weakness, heed the words of Brother Wilcox: "When you feel like you have failed too many times to keep trying, remember Christ's Atonement and the grace it makes possible are real."[131]

For the times you can't see grace because your circumstances, Brother Wilcox said,

> As dark as our trials, sins, and mistakes may appear, we can always have confidence in the grace of Jesus Christ. Do we earn a sunrise? No. Do we have to be worthy of a chance to begin again? No. We just have to accept these blessings and take advantage of them. As sure as each brand-new day, grace—the enabling power of Jesus Christ—is constant.[132]

Grace is real. It is constant.

If you can't feel it now, choose to believe it is still there and open your arms a little wider. Ask God to help you see it. Ask a trusted spouse, family member, friend, or Church leader to help you recognize it in your life. Because it is there.

Adam Miller suggests that maybe "we don't have to work our way into grace; we have to stop working so hard to pretend we aren't already in it."[133] This can take many forms, like taking credit for God's grace, seeking validation for victimhood, and simple straight up denial.

130 Neil A. Anderson, *Wounded,* General Conference (Salt Lake City: The Church of Jesus Christ of Latter-day Saints), October 2018, Gospel Library App.

131 Bradley R. Wilcox, *Worthiness Is Not Flawlessness*, General Conference (Salt Lake City: The Church of Jesus Christ of Latter-day Saints), October 2021, Gospel Library App.

132 Bradley R. Wilcox, *His Grace is Sufficient,* BYU Speeches delivered July 12, 2011, accessed May 1 2023, https://speeches.byu.edu/talks/brad-wilcox/his-grace-is-sufficient/.

133 Adam S. Miller, *Future Mormon: Essays in Mormon Theology* (Salt Lake City: Greg Kofford Books, Inc.), 2016.

The Savior promised He would not leave us comfortless. Through His grace, He will come to us (see John 14:18), to you.

I'll admit, there were times when I struggled with my daughter, Grace. Moments I felt lost, helpless, and even angry. Moments I didn't feel His grace.

But, as I look back, I can see His grace woven through every memory, lighting dark moments and lifting heavy burdens. His grace was the love of writing I rediscovered just two years before my daughter came to our home. Over the years, writing has been soul-filling and God-connecting.

His grace was in the times I turned to Him in my frustration rather than away from Him. His grace was in the answers I had and the apologies I gave. His grace was in the people He sent into her life and mine. His grace was in the tender way He didn't judge when I struggled and the strong way He lifted me when I fell. His grace was in the deep breaths and second and third and fourth do-overs. His grace was in chances lost that turned out to be opportunities gained. His grace held me when I thought I was shedding tears alone.

So many times I didn't see grace, but it was there.

I believe grace is with me always. I look for it in the dark and in the light. Sometimes it's apparent and when it's not, I look for it and assume it's there.

I believe in God's grace. I love God's grace.

It runs through me, sustains me, and transforms me.

Some people run on caffeine. I run on grace.

So, if you can't see grace right now, it's okay. It's still there, like the sun behind a layer of clouds, shining brightly. Whether your local cloud coverage comes from doubt, guilt, shame, fear, grief, or sorrow, know that it is temporary and grace is still there. I echo the words of Brother Wilcox.

> As dark as our trials, sins, and mistakes may appear, we can always have confidence in the grace of Jesus Christ. Do we earn a sunrise? No. Do we have to be worthy of a chance to begin again? No. We just have to accept these blessings and take advantage of them.

As sure as each brand-new day, grace—the enabling power of Jesus Christ—is constant.[134]

Whether or not your life (your family, your job, your body, your friends, your faith, your calling, etc.) looks like you thought it would, as you go to your Father for help, He will give you grace to make it what He knows it can be.

Because grace is there.

I chose to start and end this chapter with my daughter, Grace, not because she was so hard, but because she was one of the vehicles for grace in my life. His grace helped me to see my daughter underneath the layers of trauma. His grace amplified the love I developed for her. His grace transformed her from a young, hurting girl to a vibrant, courageous woman. His grace did that. And He allowed me to be a part of it. He changed her and changed me in the process.

God's grace changes problems, possibilities, and people. It is the power by which we breathe, heal, and learn. Through grace we are forgiven and transformed.

All we need to do is give Him our sufficient, and He will give us His. And we can be whole now and forever. This is His plan. This is grace.

134   Bradley R. Wilcox, *His Grace is Sufficient,* BYU Speeches delivered July 12, 2011, accessed May 1 2023, https://speeches.byu.edu/talks/brad-wilcox/his-grace-is-sufficient/.

CHAPTER 8

Sufficient Strength

God's grace gives me reason to be an optimist. Yes, life has its challenges, and we could so easily choose to focus on and get bogged down by them. But, even in my most challenging times, grace is present. That means God is present. Jesus is present. When I focus on the fact that the all-powerful, all-knowing, all-loving Father and my Savior are present in my life in every moment, it is hard to be a pessimist. When I think of all the help I'm offered through God's grace because of Jesus's Atonement, optimism shines.

Grace is sufficient for all the things we need to transform. We give Him our sufficient at the same time He gives us His. He gives us everything we need to survive and thrive. He makes us whole.

Grace also makes us strong.

Recognizing this can help us proclaim the words of President Spencer W. Kimball: "There are great challenges ahead of us, giant opportunities to be met. I welcome that exciting prospect and feel to say to the Lord, humbly, 'Give me this mountain', give me these challenges."[135]

And man, do we have mountains to climb that require effort and faith! But it is on these mountains we find God. With His help, we can climb to places we otherwise couldn't and see things we otherwise wouldn't.

---

135   Spencer W. Kimball, *Give Me This Mountain*, General Conference (Salt Lake City: The Church of Jesus Christ of Latter-day Saints,) October 1979, Gospel Library App.

Nephi had many mountains to climb. Things like leaving his life-long home and belongings, as well as gaining a testimony of his father's prophethood and the Savior. He was asked to do some hard things. Like when, after two failed attempts to get the brass plates from Laban, Nephi was faced with two angry brothers and a job still undone. Laman and Lemuel were furious and violent, and wanted to give up. Despite a visit from a literal angel, they doubted God and themselves. I love Nephi's response.

> *Let us go up* again unto Jerusalem, and *let us be faithful* in keeping the commandments of the Lord; for behold he is mightier than all the earth, then why not mightier than Laban and his fifty, yea, or even than his tens of thousands? Therefore, let us go up; *let us be strong.*"[136]

Laban had tried to kill them. Laman and Lemuel had just beaten Nephi and Sam with a rod. And still, Nephi said, "give me this mountain." How could he be so determined and so optimistic? Because he knew that if God asked His children to do something, "he shall prepare a way for them that they may accomplish the thing which he commanded them."[137]

And so, he went back on his metaphorical mountain and "being a man large in stature, and also having received much strength of the Lord,"[138] he continued to climb, and he succeeded.

Nephi understood the enabling and strengthening power of grace. He knew his sufficient coupled with God's sufficient was sufficient for the task.

We each have our own mountains to climb. Relationships, financial matters, addiction recovery, building beliefs, family ties, chronic and acute illness, and more. Each has challenging steep ascents. Each offers beautiful vistas. And all include grace. Divine help is ours if we want it in every day, every minute, every moment.

Can you feel the optimism growing?

If I could debunk a saying that's still widely used, it would be this one: "God doesn't give us anything we can't handle." This simply isn't true. We aren't meant to conquer this life alone. We aren't equipped

136   1 Nephi 4:1-2 italics added.
137   1 Nephi 3:7.
138   1 Nephi 4:31.

to. That's not a surprise to God. That is part of His plan. Remember, grace *is* the plan.

As a kid in the 70's, watching reruns on TV was the best. Among my favorites were *The Brady Bunch, Gilligan's Island, the Monkees,* and *Gidget.*

Gidget, played by the brilliant Sally Field, was an enthusiastic yet naïve teenager in the 60's trying to figure life out. Sometimes her problems were small, other times they were mountains. During a conversation with her dad one day, Gidget lamented, "Oh Dad, why can't the world ever be the way you want it to be?"

With love in his eyes, her dad replied, "Then little girls would never come to their fathers for consolation."[139]

What if we asked God the same question? "Oh Father, why can't the world ever be the way I want it to be?" I could see Him answering: "Then My children would never come to Me for help."

We are not meant to have charmed lives free of difficulties, discomfort, pain, or effort. We are not meant to meet the challenges alone. We are not meant to climb these mountains alone.

We *are* meant to need our Father, to go to Him. We are meant to need grace and to use it. We are meant to need and use the strength that comes from grace. Needing and receiving His strength *is* the plan.

This is great news because we have a work to do, my friends, and we could use the help. We have people to minister to, families to raise, responsibilities to fulfill, talents to nurture, callings to magnify, testimonies to strengthen, opportunities to seize, and challenges to overcome.

We know the plan. We can make and keep covenants. We have access to the grace and power wrought through the Atonement of Jesus Christ. We have His gospel and His invitation to take part in His Kingdom. We have light to share, divine laws to obey, and connections to make.

And we have all the help we need. Paul taught us that "God is able to make all grace abound toward you; that ye, always, having all

---

139   *Gidget,* Season 1 Episode 7, "Gidget Is a Proper Noun," directed by Oscar Rudolph, aired Oct. 27, 1965, on ABC, https://www.imdb.com/title/tt0588013/.

sufficiency in all things, may abound to every good work."[140] That right there is reason to hope and rejoice! Like Paul, we can do all things through Christ and His grace.[141]

"Give us these mountains!" we say with optimism then. Give us the life we fought to have in premortality. Give us the joy and the successes and the trials. Give us these mountains, for on them we find strength, we find grace, we find Him.

Sufficient Strength

Back in the days when my hair was big and my waist was small, around 1991, I went on date with a guy that would change my life's trajectory. I don't remember the guys' name, but I clearly remember two things. He had a delicious British accent, and he took me to a small live musical called *A Day, a Night, and a Day*. I was mesmerized by both. But it was the musical that moved me most.

It was the first musical written by Doug Stewart, the mind behind the cult-classic *Saturday's Warrior*. With music by the brilliant William Marsden, the story of a group of believers in Christ came to life for me.

Taken from the Book of Mormon, the musical starts with Samuel the Lamanite prophesying of the impending birth of the Savior. The sign? A day, a night, and a day of light in five years' time. Most people didn't believe him. Some even tried to kill him. But there was group of people who did believe.

Fast forward five years to the time the sign was to come to pass, and it hadn't. Stewart creates a beautiful cast around the real character of Nephi, the son of Nephi and the prophet at that time. Despite the "signs and greater signs and greater miracles wrought among the people,"[142] some began to mock the believers for their faith.

The scriptures don't give details of the struggle of the faithful aside from saying "the people who believed began to be very sorrowful, lest by any means those things which had been spoken might not come to pass."[143]

---

140   2 Corinthians 9:8.
141   see Philippians 4:13.
142   3 Nephi 1:4.
143   3 Nephi 1:7.

I think the term "very sorrowful" might be one of the most understated expressions in scriptures. You see, those who didn't believe had chosen a day that, unless the sign came to pass—that day, night, and day of light—all the believers who would not deny they believed in Jesus Christ would be killed.

Spoiler alert, the sign came. The musical was phenomenal. And I was in love. Not with the British guy, but the show. My date had friends in the cast whom I met at an after-show get-together. After hitting it off with one of the leads, a madly talented singer, she and I hatched a plan. I would audition for the show, and we'd be roommates.

Our plan worked. Somehow, I got an ensemble role. And somehow, we found a place to rent so I wouldn't have to keep driving from Provo to Salt Lake four times a week.

Watching the show was one thing, but being in it was another. Aside from the black spandex unitard I donned for a dance scene with moves I always forgot and a *Dirty Dancing* style lift I could never perfect, I loved every moment on stage in the chorus.

Instead of watching the believers sing with Nephi of their faith in the face of death, I was singing those words. I felt just a small taste of what they might have felt. What faith they must have had to testify of Jesus knowing that a simple denial of Him—just a few words—would save their lives.

The believers and unbelievers alike had seen the same prophecy five years before. "There were great signs given unto the people, and wonders; and the words of the prophets began to be fulfilled. And angels did appear unto men, wise men, and did declare unto them glad tidings of great joy, thus in this year the scriptures began to be fulfilled."[144]

So, what made some believe and others not? "Nevertheless, the people began to harden their hearts, all save it were the most believing part of them . . . and began to depend upon their own strength and upon their own wisdom."[145]

The difference was the strength they relied on.

Despite their sorrow, the believers relied on the strength of the Lord and "they did watch steadfastly for that day and that night and

144   Helaman 16:13-14.
145   Helaman 16:15.

that day which should be as one day as if no night, that they might know their faith had not been in vain."[146]

Can you imagine what that must have been like? How strong was their faith and their conviction. These weren't just random people, but real people with families, hopes, dreams, jobs, cares, and loved ones. With one denial, they would have been spared. But they stayed strong. God gave them strength.

One night, during one of my last performances, I had a moment of clarity and empathy. Though in the ensemble, the director had asked me to wrap my arms around a young boy, a son, while we sang a plea to God to give us faith as we waited for the sign. I cried. The tears weren't acting. They were real. The strength it must have taken for them to keep their eyes on Christ, to not give into fear, to be willing to offer themselves and perhaps even their children as a sacrifice to that faith was overwhelming.

I cried because I felt that plea myself. I was struggling to find my way. I didn't feel I was a particularly awesome person. I made mistakes. I felt weak. And I needed help. I needed His grace. I needed strength. His strength.

The sign did come for the believers. The star appeared, lighting the sky (and stage) as bright as the day. Through the speakers, the words of the Savior given to the prophet Nephi the day before were sung, "Lift up your head . . . I come into the world."[147] And I felt it. I felt His love and His strength. I felt *Him*.

Apparently, I felt Him too much, because the next day the director taught me a new word: "overacting." He asked me to give it a little less effort the next show. I didn't tell the director why there was more that night. In fact, I didn't tell anyone. I kept it close to my heart and let it work its magic. But I digress.

This group of brave believers are not alone. The scriptures are filled with stories of good people made stronger by grace. And God gave it every time.

Moroni is one such person. When he is concerned about his weakness in writing, he turns to the Lord who assures him, "my grace is

---

146   3 Nephi 1:8.
147   3 Nephi 1:14.

sufficient for all men that humble themselves before me; for if they humble themselves before me, and have faith in me, then will I make weak things become strong unto them."[148]

God can make us strong! Strong enough to face life, death, and everything in between.

There is a process, however, to obtaining His strength. It can be found in our efforts to have sufficient hope, faith, humility, and repentance. Elder Craig D. Cardon confirmed that "if we exercise faith in the Lord Jesus Christ, the enabling power of His Atonement *strengthens* us in our moment of need."[149]

Elder Ulysses Soares shared a similar sentiment when he said,

> as we draw nearer to [the Savior], surrendering ourselves spiritually to His care, we will be able to take upon ourselves His yoke, which is easy, and His burden, which is light, thus finding that promised comfort and rest. Furthermore, we will receive the strength we all need to overcome the hardships, weaknesses, and sorrows of life, which are exceedingly difficult to endure without His help and healing power."[150]

The Lord can and does give us the strength we need to accomplish the things He wants us to accomplish. When Joseph Smith was commanded to translate the plates, the Lord said, "I have given my servant Joseph sufficient strength,"[151] to do what needed to be done. This strength can manifest in external or internal ways.

When I was seventeen, I fell asleep at the wheel while driving home from a dance. It took only a fraction of a second of the slapping of the palm tree fronds in the highway meridian to wake me up. God gave me the strength of clarity in that moment. My mind moved so fast that everything around me seemed slow. I never panicked, but, as I pulled the steering wheel to the side, I overcorrected. The car spun to the right and kept spinning. I wondered if this was how I was going to die.

148   Ether 12:27.

149   Craig A. Cardon, *The Savior Wants to Forgive*, General Conference (Salt Lake City: The Church of Jesus Christ of Latter-day Saints), April 2013, Gospel Library App.

150   Ulisses Soares, *Jesus Christ: The Caregiver of Our Soul*, General Conference (Salt Lake City: The Church of Jesus Christ of Latter-day Saints), April 2021, Gospel Library App.

151   D&C 9:12.

As the car spun across four empty lanes, I had a conversation with myself about life and the changes I needed to make before it landed backwards in a ditch. Breathing steady and wide awake now, I saw one car unknowingly pass by. Then I heard the instruction to flash my headlights at the next car. I did. They pulled over. It was a police car. As they approached the passenger window, I had the mental clarity to tell them I was okay and ask for a ride home. They were amazed at my physical and mental state. I was alright. They told me I should be dead. By God-given grace and strength, I wasn't.

Now, lest you think I function in a continual state of mental strength and clarity, may I refer you back to chapter two when I, with a touch of melodrama, prepared to meet God. Also, I have been known to cry out of frustration when I have lost my keys. My mental and emotional strength may not be consistent, but God's strength is consistent and sufficient.

His strength can be manifested in physical ways as well. Like the time I broke my leg while hiking with a group of young women in an underground lava tube. The only way out was to hike three quarters of a mile on a broken leg. While pulling on my husband's backpack, God gave me the strength to limp, scoot, and pull myself out of that cave. During the appointment with the orthopedic specialist, he told me my ankle and leg were broken and he had no idea how I walked out on my leg. He said it was a miracle. It *was* a miracle—the miracle of strength given through grace.[152]

The beautiful bottom line is that God can give us strength sufficient for our needs. Sometimes those needs are big, sometimes they are small, but they are all important to Him.

What is important is to remember where our strength comes from. Like the believers awaiting the sign, we can watch steadfastly for Christ, looking for Him in the scriptures, through prayer and worship, as we serve, and as we love. We can choose to be strong and then lean into the strength He gives us. It is good. It is strong. And it is so beautifully sufficient.

---

152   For the full story, see Michelle Wilson, "A Walk Out of Darkness," *Liahona*, August 2023.(United States and Canada section in the Gospel Library App.)

Weak Things Become Strong

If you were feeling like we should have spent more time in the well-loved and oft-quoted Ether 12:27, you are absolutely right. In four short sentences, this verse changes us from lost cases to conquerors. Not because of us, but because of grace. Weak things can be made strong through Jesus Christ. This is liberating news!

But this news comes with a scary caveat. To have our weaknesses turned into strengths, we have to see them. Like, *really* see them.

The way I see it, we often deal with this dilemma in one of three different ways. Sometimes, we see our weaknesses as proof we are not good enough, that we are failing God. Then our weaknesses and short-comings elicit feelings of guilt, fear, and even shame.

Another way we sometimes choose to deal with our weaknesses is to refuse to see them. Denial can be a much more comfortable vacation spot. Pride, shame, or fear are often the reasons we won't look at our weaknesses. Either we've told ourselves we are too good to have them, or if we do, they are someone else's fault, or we try to hide them from ourselves and others. We can even try to hide them from God.

The third option is to do what the Lord suggests in our favorite verse:

> And *if men come unto me* I will show unto them their weakness. I give unto men weakness that they may be humble; and my grace is sufficient for all men that humble themselves before me; for if they humble themselves before me, and have faith in me, then will I make weak things become strong unto them.[153]

When we choose this third option, the Lord helps us see our weaknesses. He sees them perfectly and will lovingly show them to us through His eyes. Then we can see our weaknesses for what they are: a product of our toddler divinity. We are unfinished gods. We are His little children. We are still growing, still figuring out who and what we want to be. We are not yet full-grown or whole.

We are still growing. And change is His plan for us.

---

153   Ether 12:27, italics added.

And so, we take the things that are weak—maybe our patience, our resolve, our perspective, or even our faith—and we let the Lord make them strong. This is where He shines.

Paul was very aware of his shortcomings and weaknesses. In a sweet and intimate exchange, Paul lamented to the Lord about a "thorn" in his flesh. He was frustrated and maybe even hurt by it. He didn't want it, so much so that he petitioned the Lord to remove it.

I love the Savior's response: "My grace is sufficient for thee: for my strength is made perfect in weakness."[154]

Isn't that wonderful? The Lord's strength is made perfect in our weakness. Or in other words, the process of changing weakness into strength requires His love and His grace. That process binds us together with Him.

To put it this way, our weaknesses give us the blessed opportunity to connect with the Savior and be one with Him. This means that I, a weak thing, can be made strong merely by entering that relationship, that process with Him. It isn't simply about changing a weakness into a strength, but changing my weak and alone state into a strong and united one.

When I understand this, I understand Paul's reaction in that same verse. He said, "Most gladly therefore will I rather glory in my infirmities, that the power of Christ may rest upon me."[155]

I want to do a fist pump into the air in an act of passionate solidarity. I mean, I still don't love my issues, but I love that they bring me to Jesus.

Then Paul took it to another level: "Therefore," he said, "I take pleasure in my infirmities, in reproaches, in necessities, in persecutions, in distresses." My fist bump falls just a bit until Paul closes with a passionate, "for Christ's sake: for when I am weak, then I am strong."[156]

And now I truly get it. I am the strongest when I take my weakness to Christ. The "then" in that verse *is* Jesus. It could read, "For when I am weak, in Jesus I am strong."

---

154   2 Corinthians 12:9.
155   Ibid.
156   2 Corinthians 12:10.

As far as I can tell, He does this in at least three ways. One, when we come to Him, we have access to His power. President Nelson said that

> God so loved the world that He sent His Only Begotten Son to help us. And His Son, Jesus Christ, gave His life for us. All so that we could have access to godly power—power sufficient to deal with the burdens, obstacles, and temptations of our day.[157]

The Lord assures us to "Fear thou not; for I am with thee: be not dismayed; for I am thy God: I will strengthen thee."[158] Here, the strength comes as we engage God in our righteous desires and actions. I like to think of this like a trampoline. We must put in the effort to move, but when we do, the foundation we are on allows us to reach higher and do more than we could on our own.

Another way the Savior turns our weaknesses into strengths is to literally do it. I watched my son go from an alright Spanish student in high school to a fluent Spanish speaker on his mission. A sweet friend of mine was asked to lead a large conference, prayed about it, and accepted the position despite doubts, insecurities, and a lack of skills. I witnessed her transform in confidence and ability that year as she leaned on the Savior for guidance and support. I have also seen, and experienced the transformation that the repentance process brings, as weakness and temptation are replaced by strength and resolve.

A third way Jesus Christ can change our weakness into strength is that He can take the parts of us that may seem negative and turn them into positives in His purposes. Consider Paul. As Saul, he has a powerful presence and a passion for his understanding of justice. The road to Damascus changes that. No, let me rephrase. The Savior changes him. As Saul learns about the Lord, he gives his full faith and devotion to Him. The Lord takes and uses Paul's powerful presence and passion for justice for His purposes. Paul transforms from an enemy of God to one of His greatest missionaries.

157   Russell M. Nelson, *Drawing the Power of Jesus Christ into Our Lives*, General Conference (Salt Lake City: The Church of Jesus Christ of Latter-day Saints), April 2017, Gospel Library App.

158   Isaiah 41:10.

It's like when my kids were little, I would sometimes see them using their talents in ways that weren't . . . optimal. Sometimes it took just a look to remind them to "use your powers for good." Other times, we'd have our own version of a road to Damascus.

We have been given wonderful gifts and talents! Things we are good at, things we enjoy. But even good things can be bad if they aren't used appropriately. A flower can be a weed if it is unwanted or grows in the wrong place.

When we approach the Lord, we can ask Him to show us our weaknesses and, with His help, they can become strengths. We can lean on His power to rise to the challenges of life. We can work hand in hand with deity to turn our weaknesses into strengths, and we can take the strengths we do have and make sure we are using them to strengthen His work.

God's grace through the sacrifice of Jesus Christ is real. It works. But only when we work together. Elder Rasband reminds us of this collaboration when he said, "The Lord is with us, mindful of us and blessing us in ways only He can do. Prayer can call down the strength and the revelation that we need to center our thoughts on Jesus Christ and His atoning sacrifice."[159]

We are hopping on a tandem bike with someone who never gets tired. It's a team effort, if you will. He pedals from behind and gives direction. We pedal along and steer the bike. We work in unison to go where He wants us to go and become who He knows we can be.

Our shortcomings are our pathway to Jesus Christ. Our weaknesses are our invitation to His strength. And our struggles are our opportunity to reach to Him and let Him lift us up.

It is a beautiful thing when you think about it! There is reason to hope and even celebrate like Paul who was "glad when we are weak, and ye [the Lord] are strong; and this also we wish, even your perfection."[160] I love the beauty of that last line. It could be said in another way: our hope is being one with You.

---

159   Ronald A. Rasband, *Be Not Troubled*, General Conference (Salt Lake City: The Church of Jesus Christ of Latter-day Saints), October 2018, Gospel Library App.
160   2 Corinthians 13:9.

That truly is our hope. And because of our weakness, it is more than a hope. It can be a magnificent reality.

The Strength of Angels

One of my favorite scenes in the Old Testament involves the prophet Elijah. Elijah does some amazing and hard things. He raises a boy from the dead, calls down fire from heaven, and causes the rain to stop falling for over three years. Despite (or maybe because of) the miracles he performs, Elijah finds himself running for his life. After a full day's journey, he has had enough. He sits down underneath a juniper tree and gives up. "It is enough; now, O Lord, take away my life."[161]

I don't claim to know what was going through his head and heart at that time, but I do know what it feels like to be at my end, to feel exhausted, to feel done.

This might look like a weak moment, but even in the throes of giving up, Elijah has the strength to turn to the Lord. Worn out, Elijah falls asleep under that tree.

I love what happens next. Elijah wakes up, not because the men chasing him find him or because of someone passing by. He wakes up because of an angel. What I love most is what the angel does. He tells him to "arise and eat"[162] a cake the angel had made while Elijah was sleeping. Tell me that is not *the* coolest angel ever.

The angel leaves. Elijah arises and eats . . . and then goes back to sleep. The angel returns and touches Elijah, again telling him to get up and eat, adding because "the journey is too great for thee."[163] Elijah, who now seems to get that the Lord still has work for him to do, arises again and "went in the strength of that meat forty days and forty nights."[164]

There are couple things I take from this account. First, the food the Lord provided gives Elijah strength far beyond what food typically provides. His power is beyond our own.

---

161   1 Kings 18:4.
162   1 Kings 19:5.
163   1 Kings 19:7.
164   1 Kings 19:8.

Another takeaway is that God knows what we need. In this moment, Elijah wants to die. God knows he needs nourishment, direction, and purpose. He also knows the best way to provide for Elijah's needs. He could have sent an old friend or a wise stranger. But the Lord sends an angel with campfire skills to his aid.

Which takes me to the third takeaway—one of the ways God gives us strength is through His angels.

Now, I've never been woken up from a Sunday nap by an angel who'd just baked me a chocolate cake. But I did have an experience that came close.

For context, after something really big happens in my life—specifically something that God has brought into my life, like an invitation, an opportunity, or an achievement—I commemorate it with a chocolate covered strawberry.

This tradition was born on May 9, 2013. I'd flown into Utah to meet with some people at Deseret Book. I walked into that meeting not sure what would happen. I walked out of the meeting with the words "we want to publish your book" still ringing in my ears. It was a magical moment that I didn't want to forget. I turned the corner and saw the Rocky Mountain Chocolate company right in front of me. I bought a chocolate covered strawberry, found a quiet table in the sun, and ate it while the angels sang. It was a date with God, of sorts.

Over the years, I've had four different occasions to eat a chocolate covered strawberry. Each one was significant in their own way, but all had something in common; they were all moments between me and God where I acknowledged Him and what He had brought to me and through me.

Recently I had another significant event come my way, a writing opportunity that felt exciting and overwhelming all at once. Though I felt an initial confirmation it was from God, the more I thought about it, the doubts began to settle in. My husband, who usually talked me down from the Cliffs of Overanalysis™, was out of cell reception for two days. First, I prayed and talked to God, specifically asking Him for a confirmation this was really what He wanted me to do, something He thought I could do. Then, I called my dad and prayed again. I really needed an answer and asked God to speak to me in a way I would understand. Then, I fell asleep on the couch.

Fifteen minutes later a knock at my door woke me up. I rubbed my eyes and answered it. There, on my welcome mat, was an unmarked box. I wondered if my husband had ordered something online and was tempted to put the box on his desk when I saw that it was addressed to me.

I set it on the kitchen table and cut the tape. Then I pulled the lid back and saw them.

A box of ten chocolate covered strawberries.

The moment I saw them, I burst into tears. I knew what they meant. I knew God was speaking to me.

What I didn't know was that the day before, a sweet friend was on a bus driving through Jordan, Israel, minding her own business when she heard the impression, "Send Michelle chocolate." Realizing how totally random that was, she shook it off. Then it came again, "Send Michelle chocolate." She acquiesced, replying that she'd send me some chocolate when she returned home to the States. "Send Michelle chocolate now," the voice said. And so, having no idea why, this good woman whipped out her phone. She remembered my mentioning my chocolate covered strawberries thing before, so there on a bus in the middle of Israel, she ordered a box of chocolate covered strawberries to be sent via next-day delivery.

I wiped my tears as I pulled one out of the box and ate it. It was ordered by my friend, but it was sent from God to commemorate this new opportunity. It was from Him to me.

Angels are real, explained Elder Holland.

> But when we speak of those who are instruments in the hand of God, we are reminded that not all angels are from the other side of the veil. Some of them we walk with and talk with—here, now, every day. Some of them reside in our own neighborhoods.[165]

And some ride buses in Jordan, Israel and order chocolates.

---

165   Jeffrey R. Holland, *The Ministry of Angels*, General Conference (Salt Lake City: The Church of Jesus Christ of Latter-day Saints), October 2008, Gospel Library App.

We have all had experiences with "angels on earth," good people that let God work through them. And most likely, we have all been earthly angels ourselves.

But I want to spend some time with heavenly angels, the kind of divine messengers that come *here* from *there* to help us and give us strength.

God has used angels since the time of Adam and Eve. The scriptures are replete with accounts of angelic visitations and ministries. So is the life of the Savior. From the angelic announcement of His birth to the announcement of His Second Coming, angels have been a part of His story. In one of the darkest hours of Jesus's life, His suffering in the Garden of Gethsemane, it is an angel that is sent to strengthen Him.[166]

Though we probably won't have as many tangible experiences with angels, Elder Holland gives us a wonderful idea of how God uses them in our lives.

> Usually such beings are *not* seen. Sometimes they are. But seen or unseen they are *always* near. Sometimes their assignments are very grand and have significance for the whole world. Sometimes the messages are more private. Occasionally the angelic purpose is to warn. But most often it is to comfort, to provide some form of merciful attention, guidance in difficult times.[167]

Angel—real angels—attend us. What a powerful source of strength God has provided for me and for you!

As we strive for sufficient hope, faith, humility, and repentance, He will give us sufficient help, sometimes even from angels. Joseph Smith assured us that "if you live up to your privileges, the angels cannot be restrained from being your associates."[168]

What if you're not sure you have angels around you to strengthen you? Elder Holland assures us "we can pray for angels to attend us."[169]

---

166   see Luke 22:43.

167   Jeffrey R. Holland, *The Ministry of Angels*, General Conference (Salt Lake City: The Church of Jesus Christ of Latter-day Saints), October 2008, Gospel Library App.

168   Henry B Eyring, *Sisters in Zion*, General Conference (Salt lake City: The Church of Jesus Christ of Latter-day Saints), October 2020.

169   Jeffrey R. Holland, *The Ministry of Angels*, General Conference (Salt Lake City: The Church of Jesus Christ of Latter-day Saints), October 2008, Gospel Library App.

And, if that wasn't bold enough, Elder Holland gave us a plain, direct, and very powerful instruction: "Ask for angels to help you."[170]

Angels are simply messengers from God. They are family and friends and others who have passed through the veil. They are connected to us. They remember us, and they love us. They have a vested interest in us, in me and in you.

Whether you are faced with a new, exciting, and maybe intimidating opportunity, or a long-term, awful, and probably unwanted trial, you have the right and privilege to receive strength from God through angels both heavenly and earthly. That boggles my mind, but it's true. Angels can and will attend you.

Can I say one more thing about angels here?

I love that as angels attend to us, we can attend to them. I remember clearly, through a priesthood blessing I received years ago, I was told there were angels assigned to assist me and they "delighted in my company." I will admit, there have been times while I'm driving when I've talked to, sung to, and even told dad jokes to the angels I'm assuming are near. I mean, if God says they are, then they must be. And why not make their day a little brighter?

Recently I took one of my ancestors named Emma to the Seattle temple for the day. First, I was baptized for her. Then confirmed. We then participated in her initiatory and attended an endowment session together. We finished the night at the altar where I knelt as her proxy as she was sealed to her parents.

After the sealing, I walked down the hall of the temple alone. Except, I wasn't alone. She was there. I *felt* her there. I extended my right hand out to my side and fully expected her to take it. That's how close she felt. It was a spiritual experience unlike any other I'd had. I didn't go to the temple to "do her work." I took her to the temple and we worked together. Me and Emma, with only the thinnest of veils between us. She was grateful, and I was strengthened.

Angels are real and they are here. We probably won't see them, but we can surely ask for them and believe they are there. Through them,

---

170   Jeffrey R. Holland, *Place No More for the Enemy of My Soul*, General Conference (Salt Lake City: The Church of Jesus Christ of Latter-day Saints), October 2010, Gospel Library App.

God can guide us, comfort us, and gives us the help we need. Through them, He can give us the strength we need to not only survive but thrive in this life. It's not only a beautiful thought; it is a beautifully sufficient truth.

We Can Do Hard Things

We truly do have a great work to do, and God has given us the access to strength sufficient to do it.

Sometimes we get caught up in how hard life can be because, well, life *can* be hard! But if we aren't careful, we can lean into our misery and the unfairness of it all. This is becoming easier to do in a society that tells us discomfort equals bad or that we are good enough with no need to challenge ourselves or grow.

Perhaps we should take a few things from the past and bring them back, like these words spoken by Eliza R. Snow, the second general Relief Society president, on October 27, 1869. To the Relief Society members of her ward, she said,

> Women should be women and not babies that need petting and correction all the time. I know we like to be appreciated but if we do not get all the appreciation which we think is our due, what matters? We know the Lord has laid high responsibility upon us, and there is not a wish or desire that the Lord has implanted in our hearts in righteousness but will be realized, and the greatest good we can do to ourselves and each other is to refine and cultivate ourselves in everything that is good and ennobling to qualify us for those responsibilities.[171]

God wants strong women. And He's got them. We are the ones who fought in the premortal life to get where we are now. We are the "noble and great ones."[172] We came to earth already equipped with talents, skills, and strengths. And now that we are here, we have access to divine

---

171   Eliza Snow, address to Lehi Ward Relief Society, October 17, 1869, Lehi Ward, Alpine (Utah) Stake, in Relief Society, Minute Book, 1868-79, Church History Library, Salt Lake City, 26-27.

172   Abraham 3:22.

strength as well. The Lord said, "I will strengthen thee; yea, I will help thee; yea, I will uphold thee with the right hand of my righteousness."[173]

Life can be hard, but our hard things can make us strong. In fact, I was chatting with a friend about trials one day when I asked her if she really thought good could come out of every trial. She thought for a moment, the said, "I don't think you can go through hard things, stay faithful, and not come out better for it."

It's true. As we are faithful, we can pass through hard things and come out changed for the better. And man, do we have help. I think of the words the Lord said to Enoch:

> Go forth and do as I have commanded thee, and no man shall pierce thee. Open thy mouth, and it shall be filled, and I will give thee utterance, for all flesh is in my hands, and I will do as seemeth me good. Behold my Spirit is upon you, wherefore all thy words will I justify; and the mountains shall flee before you, and the rivers shall turn from their course; and thou shalt abide in me, and I in you; therefore walk with me.[174]

"Walk with me." This is the epitome of *sufficient*. We walk with Him as we strive for our sufficient and as He gives us His. We both have parts to play, things to accomplish.

We can do hard things when we do them with Heavenly Father and Jesus Christ.

Paul testifies of this when he says,

> Not that I speak in respect of want: for I have learned, in whatsoever state I am, therewith to be content. I know both how to be abased, and I know how to abound: every where and in all things am instructed both to be full and to be hungry, both to abound and to suffer need. *I can do all things through Christ which strengtheneth me.*[175]

Paul is strong and the Lord makes him stronger.

I wonder if Paul thought about Joshua when he said this. Did Joshua, who lead Israel into Canaan after the departure of Moses, serve as inspiration? Joshua's must have been a daunting task, to say the least. Rather than send an angel to comfort Joshua, the Lord chooses

173   Isaiah 41:10.
174   Moses 6:32, 34.
175   Philippians 4:11–13.

a different route. He speaks to him directly: "Be strong and of good courage," He says, "only be thou strong and very courageous."[176]

What gives Joshua the courage to stay strong? The Lord answers, "Be strong and of a good courage; be not afraid, neither be thou dismayed: for the Lord thy God is with thee withersoever thou goest."[177]

Joshua's strength and courage is amplified as he walks with the Lord in a divine, covenant relationship where grace and strength flow freely.

We can do hard things with Jesus Christ.

He beckons us to "awake, awake; put on thy strength."[178]

His strength is *sufficient* for us. He can take our weaknesses and make them strengths. He can take our strengths and make them stronger. He can send earthy and spiritual angels to help.

He believes in us. Even when we don't feel strong, He can see our strength. And He knows, with His help, we can do not only hard things, but *all* things He asks us to.

We can believe in Him too, in His love, His grace, and His strength. And with optimism and great love in return, we can stand, sit, or even kneel and say, "Give me this mountain. Give me these challenges. Because I climb this mountain with you."

176   Joshua 1:6-7.
177   Joshua 1:9.
178   Isaiah 52:1.

Chapter 9

Sufficient Remembrance

My mom had many talents, one of which was needlework. She created amazing things with a needle and thread. After my mom passed, I inherited a cross-stitch piece of hers which read, "Sufficient are the stitches that, when sewn together, make a whole."

We've talked a lot about sufficient in this book. I mean, a lot. In fact, for fun, how many times do you think you've read the word *sufficient* so far? 30? 75? 192? If you guess higher, you're on the right track.

Up to this point, the word *sufficient* has entered your mind 247 times, and there is more to come.

Each mention of *sufficient* had a purpose, but when we bring them all together here, that purpose becomes whole. We see how each mention relates to one another—not in a linear way, but how they collectively weave in and out of each other, adding color to each one. Hope feeds faith. Humility leads to repentance. Repentance can evoke hope. Humility can ignite faith. They move with and through each other like school of fish swimming in crystal blue water.

When we have sufficient hope, faith, humility, and repentance collectively, we see the whole beautiful picture: We see ourselves standing next to Jesus Christ. Here, obligation is replaced by motivation, anxiety is replaced by excitement, guilt is replaced by grace, and shame is replaced by love.

Here, where our *sufficient* and His *sufficient* meet, we find peace, perspective, strength, and transformation. We find Him and we find ourselves.

The principle of *sufficient* is powerful, and one I hope I never forget.

But, I'll admit, there have been times while I've been studying and writing about *sufficient* when I have forgotten about *sufficient*, times when I've fallen back into the mindset of *enough*.

For example, I received a blessing of comfort recently where I was told to "go to the temple more to strengthen my faith." My first response was frustration. I attend the temple at least once a month already. Wasn't I doing enough? And my faith is strong. Wasn't I faithful enough? I thought I was doing okay and now He's telling me to do more. I left feeling frustrated with God and myself.

After stewing about this for a few hours, I suddenly realized what I was doing. I had listened to the blessing with the ears of *enough*. I interpreted what was said as though I wasn't doing *enough*, that I wasn't *enough*. It was a very self-centric view. The realization startled me.

I said a prayer, then considered again what I was told in my blessing: "go to the temple more to strengthen my faith." Then I looked at the words through the Savior-centric lens of *sufficient* and realized Heavenly Father wasn't reprimanding me; He was inviting me to His house so *He* could strengthen my faith. A gentle warmth confirmed my correct interpretation.

Funny how the same words could be seen as a condemnation or an invitation depending on the lens I chose to look through. It's also funny how quickly I forgot about *sufficient* and reverted to *enough*.

Since then, I've made a more concerted effort each day to examine my hope, faith, humility, and repentance. Are they *sufficient* to move me toward Jesus Christ? Am I growing closer to Him? Am I connecting with Heavenly Father? Do I pray for and receive Their help, Their grace, Their strength? Do I remember to look at myself and life through the lens of *sufficient*?

Sufficient Remembrance

Remembering things, even important things, can be hard. I read somewhere that your brain needs to hear or read a piece of information thirty times before it can be stored in your long-term memory. We have to make a purposeful effort to remember. This isn't a "me" or "you" problem or even a "now" problem. It's a human problem that's been around a long time.

Alma preaches remembrance to his people. He says,

> And now behold, I say unto you, my brethren, you that belong to this church, have you sufficiently retained in remembrance the captivity of your fathers? Yea, and have you sufficiently retained in remembrance [the Lord's] mercy and long-suffering towards them? And moreover, have ye sufficiently retained in remembrance that he has delivered their souls from hell?"[179]

What do we need to sufficiently remember?

Remember that we are not enough for people or self-perfection, nor were we ever supposed to be.

Remember that the lens of *enough* can be self-centric and the lens of *sufficient* is Savior-centric.

Remember that hope in Jesus Christ is the foundational layer of testimony.

Remember that faith in Jesus Christ is our love and belief in action.

Remember that humility isn't about shame, but about knowing who we are and who God is and feeling peace.

Remember that repentance is the breaking free of sin and running toward the Savior.

Remember that God's grace is totally and completely *sufficient* for you.

Remember the things we've been asked to do and trust that God will give us the internal/external and earthly/heavenly strength to do it.

Remember that it takes effort to remember the lens of *sufficient*.

And remember just how much Heavenly Father and Jesus Christ love us. We are Their work and Their glory. They want us to be one with Them, united and whole.

---

179   Alma 5:6.

Sustained Sufficiency

Remembering is vital. So, how do we retain a sufficient remembrance of *sufficient*?

We pray, we analyze, we practice, and pray again.

Through daily prayer, we can do an inventory of our hope, faith, humility, and repentance. Are they each *sufficient* in drawing us closer to Christ? If not, we readjust and move toward Him again.

As we pray, we can work with God to clearly see the *why* behind our discipleship in action—are we reading the scriptures, attending our meetings, magnifying our callings, going to the temple, or ministering because *we* are trying to make us *enough*? Or because we are trying to come to Christ so *He* can change us and perfect us?

As we do this over and over, our moments of *sufficient* knit together into a sustained sufficiency that grows. Elder Uchtdorf explained it this way:

> "Do you want to change the shape of your life?
>
> Change the shape of your day.
>
> Do you want to change your day? Change this hour.
>
> *Change what you think, feel, and do at this very moment.*
>
> A small rudder can steer a large ship.
>
> Small bricks can become magnificent mansions.
>
> Small seeds can become towering sequoias.
>
> Minutes and hours well spent are the building blocks of a life well lived. They can inspire goodness, lift us from the captivity of imperfections, and lead us upward to the redemptive path of forgiveness and sanctification.[180]

Moments of *sufficient* are the building blocks of a relationship well-loved and yes, a life well lived. When we spend our lives wanting to hope in Him, have faith in Him, have humility before Him, and repenting because of Him, we will have spent our lives focused on

180   Deiter F Uchtdorf, Daily Restoration, General Conference (Salt Lake City: The Church of Jesus Christ of Latter-day Saints), October 2021, italics added.

moving toward and being with the Savior. And move toward and with Him we must. President Eyring warned,

> As the forces around us increase in intensity, whatever spiritual strength was once sufficient will not be enough. And whatever growth in spiritual strength we once thought was possible, greater growth will be made available to us. Both the need for spiritual strength and the opportunity to acquire it will increase at rates which we underestimate at our peril.[181]

Change is the name of the game. Brother Wilcox reminded us that "God loves us as we are, but He also loves us too much to leave us this way."[182] Our sufficiency moves with us. As we continue to remember to live life through the lens of sufficient, we'll find that as we grow stronger, our sufficiency does too. It changes as we change. It isn't about a set measurable amount, but what is needed right now to move us closer to Jesus, over and over again.

Remember, you will make mistakes, but, as Elder Holland so beautifully expressed, "with the gift of the Atonement of Jesus Christ and the strength of heaven to help us, we *can* improve, and the great thing about the gospel is we get credit for *trying,* even if we don't always succeed."[183]

I love that sometimes simply trying *is* our *sufficient!*

It's a beautiful thing, isn't it? How small and sometimes big *sufficient* moments stitched together make a perfect *sufficient* whole. How through *sufficient* moments and His *sufficient* grace, we can be made whole.

I hope I never forget that.

---

181 Henry B. Eyring, *Always*, BYU Speeches delivered on January 3, 1999. Accessed February 28, 2024. https://speeches.byu.edu/talks/henry-b-eyring/always/.

182 Bradley R. Wilcox, *Worthiness is not Flawlessness*, General Conference (Salt Lake City: The Church of Jesus Christ of Latter-day Saints), October 2021, Gospel Library App.

183 Jeffrey R. Holland, *Tomorrow the Lord Will Do Wonders among You*, General Conference (Salt Lake City: The Church of Jesus Christ of Latter-day Saints), April 2016, Gospel Library App.

Perfect in Christ

Though *sufficient* is woven through every page of this book, I chose the title *Perfect in Christ*. Why? Because as wonderful a principle *sufficient* is, it is merely a means to an end. To *the* end.

The end is perfection in Jesus Christ—to be one with Him now and forever.

As we let go of our self-centric lens, we can let go of the false expectations that come with perfectionism. And as we hold tightly to our Savior-centric lens, we can rise to His expectations that lead to perfection in Him.

This is what it's all about, becoming whole, transformation, complete, like Him.

My friend, Jesus Christ lived for you. He died for you. He rose for you. His life is *you*.

I hope you can find your way to Him as you seek for your *sufficient*. I hope you feel the weight of *enough* lifted. And I hope you find joy in the things He would give to you.

I hope you let Him help you see yourself, love yourself, and challenge yourself. I hope you let Him help you, heal you, strengthen you, and change you.

Jesus Christ and Heavenly Father love you. They don't want you to try to be perfect alone. They want you to be perfected by being with Them. This is what they want, all They want.

You don't need to be *enough* for Them because you are everything to Them.

I hope you always remember that.

About the Author

Michelle Wilson is a wife, mom, speaker, and author of inspirational nonfiction, children's literature, and women's fiction. On the inspirational front, Michelle speaks and writes to women and young women, striving to help them access confidence, peace, and joy as they strengthen themselves and their relationships with God and others.

Michelle teaches gospel truths and empowering life principles with love and humor. She knows what it's like to be weighed down by guilt, shame, comparison, and self-doubt. She also knows how to be freed from those burdens and finds joy in sharing what she's learned with others. She loves laughter, sisterhood, family, optimism, and, most of all, her Father in Heaven and her Savior, Jesus Christ.

Scan the QR code
to visit michellewilsonwrites.com
and discover more content from Michelle.